Condorcet

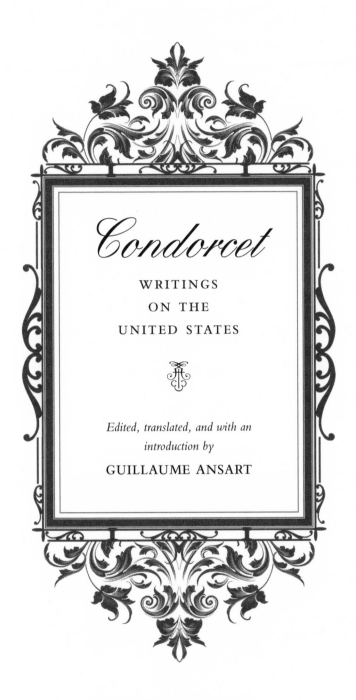

Condorcet

WRITINGS
ON THE
UNITED STATES

Edited, translated, and with an
introduction by

GUILLAUME ANSART

The Pennsylvania State University Press
University Park, Pennsylvania

Library of Congress Cataloging-in-Publication Data

Condorcet, Jean-Antoine-Nicolas de Caritat, marquis de, 1743–1794.
[Selections. English. 2012]
Condorcet : writings on the United States / translated, edited,
and with an introduction by Guillaume Ansart.
p.   cm.
Includes bibliographical references and index.
Summary: "An English translation of the writings of French
constitutional theorist Nicolas de Condorcet (1743–1794) on
the United States. Subjects include the American Revolution,
federal Constitution, and the emerging political culture in the
United States"—Provided by publisher.
ISBN 978-0-271-05381-3 (cloth : alk. paper)
1. United States—Politics and government—1775–1783—
Early works to 1800.
2. United States—History—Revolution, 1775–1783—
Influence—Early works to 1800.
3. Constitutional history—United States—Early works to 1800.
I. Ansart, Guillaume, 1960–   .
II. Title
III. Title: Writings on the United States.

JK116.C75   2012
973.3'1—dc23
2011048007

The Pennsylvania State University Press is a member of the
Association of American University Presses.

It is the policy of The Pennsylvania State University Press to
use acid-free paper. Publications on uncoated stock satisfy
the minimum requirements of American National Standard
for Information Sciences—Permanence of Paper for
Printed Library Material, ANSI z39.48-1992.

This book is printed on Natures Natural,
which contains 50% post-consumer waste.

CONTENTS

Translator's Note and Acknowledgments / *vii*

INTRODUCTION: CONDORCET AND AMERICA / *1*

Influence of the American Revolution on Europe (1786) / *21*
Introduction
Chapter One: Influence of the American Revolution on the
Opinions and Legislation of Europe
Chapter Two: On the Benefits of the American Revolution with
Respect to the Preservation of Peace in Europe
Chapter Three: Benefits of the American Revolution with
Respect to the Perfectibility of the Human Race
Chapter Four: On the Good That the American Revolution Can Do,
Through Trade, to Europe and to France in Particular
Conclusion

Supplement to Filippo Mazzei's *Researches
on the United States* (1788) / *43*

*Ideas on Despotism: For the Benefit of Those Who Pronounce
This Word Without Understanding It* (1789) / *63*

*Eulogy of Franklin: Read at the Public Session of the Academy
of Sciences, November 13, 1790* (1790) / *79*

APPENDIX: Notes to the French Translation of John Stevens's
Observations on Government (1789) / *109*

Chronology / *119*
Notes / *125*
Selected Bibliography in English / *141*
Index of Proper Names / *145*

The present translations are based on my own French edition of the same texts (Paris: Classiques Garnier, forthcoming). Proper names have been modernized to conform to current usage. I have also consulted existing translations:

"Condorcet's *The Influence of the American Revolution on Europe*." Translated and edited by Durand Echeverria. *William and Mary Quarterly* 25, no. 1 (1968): 85–108.

On the Influence of the American Revolution on Europe (intro. and chap. 1 only). In Condorcet, *Selected Writings*, edited by Keith M. Baker, 71–83. Indianapolis: Bobbs-Merrill, 1976.

"Supplement" (abr.). In Philip Mazzei, *Researches on the United States*, translated and edited by Constance D. Sherman, 383–402. Charlottesville: University Press of Virginia, 1976.

The footnotes referenced by Roman numerals are by Condorcet; those at the back of the book and indicated by Arabic numerals are my own.

Finally, I thank my wife, Dorothy Ansart, who read the entire manuscript and made countless suggestions for improvement.

Condorcet (1743–94), the last of the great figures of the French Enlightenment, was a fervent *américaniste*, one of the most prominent among the many French intellectuals who greeted American independence with unmitigated approval.[1] His writings on the United States are in some measure a reflection of their time. Late eighteenth-century France, particularly the progressive intelligentsia known as the "philosophes"—the rationalist, liberal, reform-minded intellectuals (writers, philosophers, scientists, members of the academies, enlightened administrators, etc.) who most actively championed the values of the Enlightenment—responded to the American Revolution with an enthusiasm that prompted the publication, during the period extending from the beginning of the rebellion in the colonies to the start of the French Revolution, of a rich body of literature on the United States. This corpus comprises essentially two types of texts: accounts written by firsthand observers of American society (volunteers, officers in the French expeditionary force, travelers, diplomats, etc.), and works more purely political or philosophical in nature, whose authors as a rule had no direct knowledge of the United States but relied instead on written or secondary sources for their information. The most important firsthand accounts of America of the period include St. John de Crèvecœur's *Lettres d'un cultivateur américain* (1784, a substantially revised French version of his 1782 *Letters from an American Farmer*); *Voyages dans l'Amérique Septentrionale* (1786) (*Travels in North America*) by the marquis de Chastellux, an officer in Rochambeau's army; and *Nouveau voyage dans les États-Unis de l'Amérique Septentrionale* (1791) (*New Travels in the United States of America*), an account of his 1788 trip to the United States by Brissot de Warville, the future Girondin leader. Representing the more purely political works are the chapters on colonial America and the American Revolution in Raynal's *Histoire philosophique et*

politique des établissements et du commerce des Européens dans les deux Indes
(1770–80) (*A Philosophical and Political History of the Settlements and Trade of
the Europeans in the East and West Indies*),[2] Mably's *Observations sur le gouvernement et les lois des États-Unis d'Amérique* (1784) (*Remarks Concerning the Government and the Laws of the United States of America*), and *Recherches historiques et
politiques sur les États-Unis de l'Amérique Septentrionale* (1788) (Historical and
political researches on the United States of North America) by the Italian
entrepreneur and diplomat, friend and neighbor of Jefferson in Virginia,
Filippo Mazzei.[3]

Condorcet's writings on the United States belong to this latter group of
texts, political works by authors who, with the notable exception of Mazzei,
had never traveled to America. Nevertheless, Condorcet, who had a good
knowledge of English, was very well-informed about American reality. To
be sure, like most French philosophes, he was ideologically predisposed to
be pro-American and to idealize the United States as a new philosophical
promised land. At the same time, he had a thorough factual knowledge of
recent American history. Numerous sources of information were at his disposal, namely, the travel literature by French authors listed above; books
and newspapers from England or the United States; and American political
documents, which were disseminated in France very rapidly—as early as
1777, French translations of the Declaration of Independence, the Articles
of Confederation, and several of the state constitutions were being published, and in 1787, the proposed text of the Federal Constitution was first
translated, only two months after it had been signed.[4] For further information, he could consult friends who had been to America, like Lafayette,
Mazzei, or Brissot, and his American contacts in Paris. Franklin made visits
to France in 1767 and 1769, before returning to Paris for a stay of nearly ten
years (1776–85), and Condorcet knew him well. Both were members of the
Royal Academy of Sciences. Condorcet was even closer to Jefferson, who
lived in Paris between 1784 and the autumn of 1789 and succeeded Franklin
as ambassador to France, and to Tom Paine, who first came to Paris in 1781
and spent much time in France from 1787 on. Paine, who had been granted
French citizenship, served in the National Convention with Condorcet in
1792/93, and both were elected to its committee charged with drafting a
new constitution.[5] As a member of the American Philosophical Society,
Condorcet also had access to colleagues in the United States with whom he
could correspond. Finally, as permanent secretary of the Academy of Sciences, he was assured a worldwide network of contacts. Of all the French

authors of the period who commented on the American Revolution, he was certainly one of the best informed. Indeed, his writings on the United States stand out as some of the most insightful of their time.

Other factors enhance the significance of these texts as well. Condorcet was the only major philosophe to live to see the French Revolution and to participate actively in it. His stature and influence as a constitutional theorist turned out to be considerable. Having gradually developed a position of radical constitutional republicanism that was equally critical of conservative reformers like Lafayette and of the terrorist politics of the Jacobins, he became a leading participant in the constitutional debates preceding the Terror. He was a member of the Legislative Assembly in 1791/92 (serving as its president in February 1792) and of the National Convention in 1792/93. Above all, he was the driving force behind the ill-fated, yet subsequently influential, draft constitution of 1793, the so-called Girondin constitution.[6]

Yet, despite the significance and influence of Condorcet's constitutional works, his reflections on the United States have been confined to relative obscurity for the past two hundred years.[7] We hope, with this volume, to help restore these important pre- and early revolutionary examples of French liberal political thought to their proper place in intellectual history. Revolutionary studies in both French and American history should benefit from this overdue reexamination. Here are works by a prominent philosophe and a leading constitutionalist that provide a clear confirmation of the impact of the American Revolution on the French Revolution. At the same time, Condorcet's observations on America point to an essential difference in orientation between the two revolutions. Montesquieu was, of course, a central reference and source of inspiration in American constitutional debates.[8] Likewise, Condorcet's writings on the United States abound in references to De l'esprit des lois (1748) (The Spirit of the Laws). But their tenor is almost invariably critical. Exploring how Condorcet, one of the most influential thinkers in late Enlightenment France, interpreted, evaluated, or criticized Montesquieu's science of politics in the context of his américaniste works should contribute to a better understanding of where the American and French Revolutions followed divergent or similar paths.

Condorcet's critical attitude toward the Montesquieuan approach to constitutional self-government was to a degree representative of the political climate in France in the late 1780s and early 1790s. While still very much admired as an implacable foe of despotism and intolerance, Montesquieu had been criticized, by Rousseau and Turgot among others, for being too respectful of established tradition and too reluctant to advocate far-reaching reforms. His clear preference, in constitutional terms, for a monarchy with a privileged nobility acting as a tempering intermediary power, also reinforced his conservative image among liberal reformers. So, by late 1789, it was clear that the English model extolled in *The Spirit of the Laws* and in Jean-Louis de Lolme's *Constitution de l'Angleterre* (1771) (*The Constitution of England*) did not seem an attractive option to most French revolutionaries.[9] After the fall of the monarchy in August 1792, those who continued to favor sweeping reforms were basically left with two alternatives, which Benjamin Constant would later call "modern" and "ancient" notions of liberty:[10] either Condorcet's resolutely modern vision of universal individual rights and progress through rational democratic politics, or a revival of communal classical ancient republicanism, combined with the Jacobin cult of nature, inspired in part by Rousseau.[11] "Ancient liberty," with Robespierre and the Montagne, eventually, but only temporarily, prevailed after the failure of the Girondin constitution in the spring of 1793. Thus Condorcet's analysis of the American Revolution, which helped him elaborate some of his constitutional principles, can be seen as anticipating a specific and crucial moment of French revolutionary politics, between the fall of the monarchy and the Terror.

Influence of the American Revolution on Europe (1786) was originally written in response to an essay contest sponsored by the Abbé Raynal, author of the *History of the East and West Indies*, on the question, "Has the discovery of America been harmful or useful to humankind?" The first and most important essay on America by Condorcet, it is remarkable for its radical universalism and its unwavering faith in the United States as an agent of progress. The text looks resolutely forward: Condorcet is less concerned with historical factors than with general political principles, less interested in the past than in the meaning of the emergence of the United States for the future of humanity.

Characteristically, the essay opens with a poetic simile depicting the human search for truth. Though quoting poetry is unusual for Condorcet, certainly one of the most salient features of his political thought is a constant preoccupation with universal values. A mathematician by training, he never lost his taste for abstraction. The overall structure of *Influence of the American Revolution on Europe* is quite revealing in this respect: the author begins by positing a set of general and universally valid political principles, and then goes on to examine how the laws and government of the United States illustrate these principles and how the same principles, as realized in the American Revolution, can influence the affairs of Europe in general, and France in particular.

Much of the introduction is devoted to a reflection on the best means to assure the collective happiness of a nation. Like most philosophes, Condorcet regarded public happiness as the ultimate measure of any government's legitimacy. For him, however, public happiness is not a relative notion dependent on climate, customs, or public opinion; it rests above all on respect for the "immutable laws of justice"—that is, on respect for a few inalienable, natural human rights. Public opinion can be prejudiced and tyrannical, and it can threaten natural rights. Condorcet shared with the physiocrats and his mentor Turgot the notion that enlightened rational public opinion is the only valid form of public opinion.[12] Only enlightened public opinion can add legitimacy to laws and political institutions, because only enlightened public opinion can help achieve the sole legitimate purpose of government: to secure for citizens the enjoyment of their natural rights. These are, in order of importance:

1. Individual freedom and security.
2. Security of property.
3. Equality before the law. Laws must be general and universal—that is, they must apply to the whole citizenry, without arbitrariness.
4. Participation in government, either directly or through representatives.[13]

It is worth noting that what defines democracy in the narrow sense, participation in government, comes last in Condorcet's short list. Indeed, "in a very populous society," he explains, "it must almost necessarily happen that the last of these rights turns out to be nearly nonexistent for the majority of the inhabitants of a country,"[14] and it "is important for public prosperity only insofar as it secures the enjoyment of the other rights."[15] Therefore, "with respect to public happiness, a republic with tyrannical laws can be far inferior to a monarchy."[16] For Condorcet, as Keith Baker points out, the laws should not be regarded as "the expression of the arbitrary will of the greatest number but as truths rationally derived from the principles of natural right. The rationality of legislation, in other words, is of more fundamental importance than the locus of legislative power."[17] Freedom, Condorcet proposes, has less to do with democracy in the limited sense of representative government than with the "rule of law," its rational character, and what we call today "civil society." Modern notions of freedom, with their emphasis on individual liberties, are thus radically different from what obtained, say, in the communal republics of antiquity. This concept is central to Condorcet's political theory: the example of ancient republics is basically irrelevant for the construction of freedom in large modern nations, mainly because the ancients had no clear knowledge of natural rights and therefore no concept of individual or civil liberties. In this respect, Condorcet is very much at odds with Rousseau, and a resolute proponent of "modern liberty."

In addition to the enjoyment of natural rights, Condorcet also identifies other, less essential means of achieving public happiness. They have to do with improving the material conditions of life and securing peace with foreign powers. Among these secondary means, one is singled out as especially important, equality in the distribution of wealth: "It is in the more equitable distribution of . . . goods that one must seek public happiness, and all civil laws, all laws relating to trade must tend to maintain or restore this equality among members of a nation, without interfering with the right of property or the legitimate exercise of freedom."[18] Here, Condorcet seems to be in agreement with Montesquieu's views on the crucial role of equality in a republic[19] and with an already long-established image of America, commonly accepted in late eighteenth-century France and most recently relayed by Raynal and Diderot's *History of the East and West Indies* and Crèvecœur's *Letters from an American Farmer*: that of an egalitarian society. Indeed, Condorcet is convinced that great inequalities of wealth inevitably lead to the emergence of privileged classes and thus de facto social and political inequality. *Letters from New Haven*, one of his most celebrated essays, concludes with the following warning: "Nowhere is a citizen in service, a worker or a farmer the equal of the very rich citizen for whom he works. Nowhere is the poor man with no self-respect the equal of the man who has received a thorough education. There are necessarily two classes of citizen wherever there are very poor people and very rich people, and republican equality cannot exist in any country where the civil, financial and commercial laws allow the existence of enduring large fortunes."[20]

In his analysis of the American Revolution, however, Condorcet directs most of his attention instead toward the more abstract—as well as more inherently connected to the enjoyment of natural rights—form of "republican" equality resulting from the absence of rigid stratification into social orders or classes (such as clergy, nobility, and third estate in Old Regime

France), with special privileges attached to certain classes.[21] He foresees that the leveling of social ranks in America will have far-reaching consequences. Aristocratic values rooted in the warlike, chivalric origins of the feudal nobility will no longer endure. A nation like the United States, without an aristocracy, will necessarily be a peaceful nation. The sense of honor will no longer be the false prerogative of a single class, but instead will be shared by the entire population.[22] Consequently, the energy or ambition of the American people will be channeled in useful directions: commerce, the sciences, the arts. In fact, Condorcet is convinced that the United States will soon be a major agent of progress and enlightenment in the world:

> America presents a country of vast dimensions where several million men live whose education has preserved them from prejudice and inclined toward study and reflection. No social distinctions exist there, no rewards for ambition which could lure these men away from the natural desire to perfect their minds . . . ; and nothing there confines a part of the human race to a state of abjection where it is doomed to stupidity and misery. Therefore, there is reason to hope that a few generations from now, America, by producing almost as many men who will be busy adding to the extent of our knowledge as all of Europe, will at least double its progress or make it twice as fast.[23]

Thus Condorcet's initial theoretical premise, that public happiness is primarily a function of the enjoyment of natural rights among socially equal citizens, finds its most complete illustration in the American Revolution and its declarations of rights. His uncompromising universalism naturally leads him to consider the American example of political freedom as far superior to the English one. To become rational, politics had to free itself from the weight of history and tradition. Some, like Raynal and Diderot in the *History of the East and West Indies*, tended to see in the United States a continuation of the long British experiment with liberty, but Condorcet preferred to underscore the radical novelty of the American experience:

> "Humankind had lost its rights, Montesquieu recovered them and gave them back to us" [Voltaire]. But it is not enough for these rights to be written in the books of philosophers and in the hearts of virtuous men, ignorant or weak men must be able to read them in the example of a great people.

America has given us this example. Its Declaration of Independence is a simple and sublime exposition of these rights, so sacred and so long forgotten. No nation has known them so well or preserved them with such perfect integrity.[24]

Thus begins the first chapter of *Influence of the American Revolution on Europe*. From the start Condorcet highlights the unique character of the new nation, the first in human history, he says, to have fully recognized the natural rights of man and to have enshrined them in its founding documents (the Declaration of Independence as well as the declarations of rights included in several state constitutions). For him, these solemn documents, which acknowledge the existence of certain fundamental, universal, and natural human rights, represented America's greatest contribution to the cause of human freedom, for they provided the best protection against tyranny, an ever-present danger even in representative governments. A declaration of rights is consequently an indispensable preamble of any free constitution. This principle is essential to Condorcet's constitutional philosophy, and he returns to it throughout his works and in another text presented here, *Ideas on Despotism*.[25]

But while the American example is unique, it also has, paradoxically, universal validity: "The example of a great people among whom the rights of man are respected is useful to all others despite differences in climate, manners, and constitutions. It shows that these rights are everywhere the same."[26] The reference to "differences in climate, manners, and constitutions" is of course a critical allusion to *The Spirit of the Laws*. To demonstrate the exemplarity of the American model, Condorcet clearly felt that he had to refute Montesquieu's relativism. This meant not only disproving Montesquieu's theory of climate[27] but also his theory of the balance of powers,[28] for both theories went against Condorcet's conviction that legislation must be the expression of pure rationality:

In observing how the Americans have based their peace and happiness on a small number of maxims which seem a candid expression of what common sense could have dictated to all men, we will stop praising these exceedingly complex mechanisms in which a multitude of parts leads to a forced, irregular and difficult operation, and so many counterweights that are said to balance each other out join together in reality to weigh down on the people. Perhaps we will perceive the futility, or rather the danger of these political subtleties that have been admired for too long, these systems designed to force the laws, and consequently truth, reason and justice, their immutable foundations, to change according to the temperature, to conform to the types of government, to the practices sanctioned by prejudice, and even to the follies adopted by each people, as if it would not have been more human, just and noble to seek in a rational legislation the means of disabusing peoples with regard to their errors.[29]

Between truth, reason, and justice on one hand, and legislation on the other, Montesquieu had introduced the refractive medium of local parameters: a good system of laws should also reflect or adapt to local circumstances. Condorcet is more confident in legislation's ability to influence and change society in the direction of universal truths. In the end, though, the principal factor for change in human history remains, he notes, the general progress of knowledge:

> Having long reflected upon the ways to improve the fate of humankind, I cannot help but think that there is really only one: accelerating the progress of enlightenment. Any other means has only a passing and limited effect. Even if we admitted that errors, fables, and legislations put together according to local prejudices instead of reason, have made some nations happy, we would also be obliged to admit that everywhere this overly praised happiness has vanished quickly, to be replaced by evils which reason has still not been able to cure after several centuries. Let men be enlightened, and soon you will see the good emerge effortlessly from the common will.[30]

This brings us to the specific lessons or benefits Europe and the rest of the world will be able to derive from the American Revolution. One of them is precisely an increase in the creation and diffusion of knowledge. Liberty and equality, we have already noted, will naturally prompt Americans to direct their ambition toward the arts and sciences. Far from showing any trace of the influence of the theory of American degeneration,[31] as did the *History of the East and West Indies*, Condorcet's essay develops an opposite argument. Inspired by his firm belief in the perfectibility of the human species and by his faith in the United States as an agent of progress, he sets forth what could be called a "theory of American regeneration," in which America is expected to become a leading contributor to the advancement of knowledge. This emphasis on progress is a major difference between Condorcet's vision of America and the common image of a land of virtue and simplicity still present in the *History of the East and West Indies* or the *Letters from an American Farmer.*

Regarding individual liberties, the American experience shows that freedom of the press and freedom of religion do not represent dangers to public order and tranquility. On the contrary, they promote a spirit of fraternity and respect for the law. Further, the United States will be a force for peace and for the development of commerce around the world. As noted above, a nation without an aristocracy, a democratic nation, will be less inclined to glorify warfare. The new republic will join Britain, Holland, and France as another great enlightened trading nation. The result will be an increase in global trade, more competition, and a lowering of prices. With regard to France in particular, America will provide an important new export market for its manufactured goods as well as a source of raw materials. And even from a purely moral point of view, the growth of commerce will be beneficial by reducing inequalities, at least within countries. But in one of the very few critical remarks on American legislation to be found in *Influence of the American Revolution on Europe*, Condorcet simply regrets that the United States still imposes taxes on commerce and thus has not become the first country to adopt a policy of total free trade.[32] The essential point, however, is that, in this respect too, American independence heralds the dawn of a new historical era. The age of liberty will also be the age of commerce. Or, as Constant would later put it, the age of commerce has replaced the age of war, and trade, not armed conflict, will necessarily be the dominant mode of relation between modern nations.[33]

In 1788 Condorcet contributed to the supplement to Mazzei's *Researches on the United States.* This supplement contains a translation of the proposed text of the Federal Constitution (1787) and Condorcet's commentary on it, the first such review to appear in France and probably in all of Europe.[34] Compared to the enthusiasm expressed in the 1786 essay, the tone of this commentary is more subdued. Condorcet's attitude remains one of support, but support without fervor. Generally speaking, he faults the new constitution for being needlessly complex, for lacking the simplicity and cohesion of the Articles of Confederation (1777).[35] He also raises specific objections to several important provisions:

- Dividing the legislative branch into two separate chambers is unnecessary and even dangerous, especially in a country without an aristocracy. Condorcet reiterates on this occasion his call for unity and simplicity in the form of government: "Every complication in the system, every distinction is harmful by nature, and can only be justified by necessity."[36] His hostility to bicameralism stems from his general opposition to Montesquieu's theory of the balance of powers and particularly from his rejection of the English constitutional model, with its division of the legislature into upper (Lords) and lower (Commons) houses. Therefore, he tends to see in bicameralism the expression of a conservative and aristocratic spirit.[37] More specifically, the House of Representatives and Senate reflect contradictory political principles. The first body will be elected by popular vote, and in it each state will have proportional representation; the second will be elected by the legislatures of the states, and in it each state will have equal representation. Thus the House of Representatives will represent the people, and the Senate the states. This is another dangerous complication in Condorcet's opinion: "It is a mistake to delude oneself into thinking that contrary principles can be reconciled. Such expedients will sometimes be useful, perhaps, as temporary remedies; they will never form the basis of a very solid structure. It is therefore necessary to decide in favor of one side or the other. Principles must be firm and certain, and everything must tend to uphold them."[38]
- The privilege of habeas corpus should never be suspended.
- Congress must be made accountable, at regular and frequent intervals, for its handling of public finances.
- Too much power is granted to the presidency. In general, Condorcet favored a weak executive branch, and considered a powerful president a threat to liberty.[39]
- Trial by jury should not be limited to criminal cases but extended to civil cases as well.

The following year, in a second commentary on the Constitution, Condorcet also objected to the omission of such an essential protection against tyranny as a declaration of rights, and added one more very significant caveat, this one regarding the power of the federal government relative to that of the states: "The federal constitution once established, as it is proposed, and having gained strength, there is no business with which Congress could not meddle, and of which it could not deprive the governments of the individual states."[40]

There is no question that the first political documents of the American Revolution, in particular the Virginia Declaration of Rights (1776),[41] the Declaration of Independence, the original constitution of Pennsylvania (1776),[42] and the Articles of Confederation, corresponded more closely to Condorcet's constitutional preferences than did the Federal Constitution of 1787. Like the first constitution of Pennsylvania, the constitutional plan proposed to the National Convention by Condorcet in 1793 features a unicameral legislature and an elected executive council.[43] The Federal Constitution, he thought, was too heavily influenced by the English system of government and by Montesquieu's theory of the balance of powers. Above all, he deeply regretted the establishment of two legislative chambers—a complexity, we have noted, he regarded as useless, even dangerous and aristocratic in spirit. The best protection against a possible tyranny of the legislature was not to be found in bicameralism, Condorcet was convinced, but in clear limits placed on legislative power by a declaration of inalienable rights and by censure from lower, local assemblies.[44] To be sure, he firmly believed that the legislative power, as the most direct expression of popular sovereignty, should be preeminent; hence his preference for a unicameral national legislature and for a weak executive council instead of a president. But he also believed, for the same reason having to do with popular sovereignty, that legislative power should be largely decentralized and that a good portion of it should reside in primary assemblies. He was therefore concerned to see the Federal Constitution grant so much power to the central institutions of government, Congress and the president, as compared to the states. And it had no declaration of rights.

Yet Condorcet's basic optimism about the United States was not fundamentally affected by these reservations, however substantial they may have been. What he had already stated in 1786 remained true: "Not all laws enacted since independence are equally just and wise. But no area of political or criminal law will present gross errors, oppressive or destructive principles."[45] Besides, once sound general principles have been solidly established, with time errors and abuses will necessarily give way to the logic of these principles: "If the Americans can be justly criticized, it is only for individual errors or old abuses that circumstances have not allowed them to correct. They will only need to be consistent to rectify them all."[46] This same idea, a defining feature of Condorcet's *américanisme*, is further developed in 1789 in the notes to *Examen du gouvernement d'Angleterre*: "The declarations of rights adopted by the various United States of America are neither complete nor methodical enough; but all the truths they contain are beyond doubt. The stroke of genius is to have put them forward. Now, reason and logic are enough to develop their consequences, go back to their true principles, and arrange both in methodical order."[47] What matters most is the recognition of natural rights; their universal extension and application will inevitably follow, sooner or later.

Condorcet wrote his final text concerning the United States on the occasion of Franklin's death in 1790, an event that caused much emotion in revolutionary France.[48] The next to last of the eulogies he penned for the Royal Academy of Sciences, and one of the longest, the *Eulogy of Franklin* is widely considered his most eloquent. Indeed, it is a remarkable piece of rhetoric in praise of the Enlightenment. In it, Condorcet effortlessly blends biographical and historical information with ample political and philosophical commentary to build a powerful manifesto expressing his convictions as philosophe and scientist. His subject, of course, was ideally suited to this purpose and he exploits it superbly. Who better than Franklin, the inventor-philosopher-humanitarian-revolutionary, to illustrate the values of the Enlightenment to which Condorcet was so passionately committed?

The biographical material selected for emphasis in the *Eulogy* is highly significant, starting with Franklin's humble beginnings. From this point of view, he appears the original self-made man, the archetype of this new, specifically American possibility. Franklin was of modest social origin, the fifteenth of seventeen children of a Boston candle maker, and had little formal education. But he was disciplined and self-reliant. Condorcet describes how, at fifteen, young Benjamin started to teach himself the craft of writing by imitating articles from the *Spectator*, the famous English journal published by Addison and Steele. Along with his professional training as a printer, this detail also points to an essential feature of Franklin's future career: his life-long involvement in the "public sphere."[49] During a first stay in London, Franklin, still very young, witnessed firsthand the development of the public sphere in England. He was so impressed by English journals and clubs, Condorcet tells us, that, upon his return to America, he founded his own journal, the *Pennsylvania Gazette*, and his own club in his adopted city of Philadelphia. At the same time, he began publishing the almanac that would later become famous as *Poor Richard's Almanack*. Several of the first pages of the *Eulogy* are devoted to these early endeavors, and Condorcet highlights the great benefits they brought to the public: "He wanted no class of citizen to remain without education, none to be doomed to receive only false ideas from books intended to pander to its credulity or feed its prejudices. A simple printer was then doing for America what the wisest governments had neglected through pride, or feared to do out of weakness."[50] Franklin was already performing a public service.

The personal qualities attributed to Franklin in the *Eulogy*—frugality, simplicity, a natural goodness, a disciplined work ethic—were those commonly associated with Americans by the intellectual circles of late eighteenth-century France. His style, conversation, and social manners are described as easy and natural. One detail illustrating Franklin's character is particularly telling: his successful negotiation with Native Americans on behalf of Pennsylvania's assembly. "Like him, they spoke only one language, that of common sense and good faith," Condorcet writes. More generally, the *Eulogy* suggests a deep unity underlying all of Franklin's achievements: behind both his discoveries in the physical sciences and his moral principles lies the same affinity with nature: "Mr. Franklin's education had not opened up for him a career in the sciences, but nature had given him a genius for them. His first attempts regarding electricity reveal that he knew very little even on that part of physics. . . . However, he soon surmised the immediate cause of electrical phenomena." And before he came to believe in the reality of natural morality, Franklin was already practicing it intuitively: "In his youth, he had carried Pyrrhonism to the very foundations of morals; the natural goodness of his heart and the soundness of his mind were his only guides, and they rarely led him astray. Later, he recognized that there was a moral science based on the nature of man, independent of all speculative opinions, preceding all conventions." The man "who had snatched from nature one of its secrets"[51] was as attuned to the moral as he was to the physical dimension of nature.

Franklin therefore rejected all dogmatic and artificial systems, whether in science, politics, moral philosophy, or religion. Finding pleasure in "applying the physical sciences to everyday life, to domestic economy," he was first and foremost a practical man, the perfect embodiment of the Enlightenment ideal according to which philosophy should never be divorced from the field of praxis. Likewise, his political career revealed an intellect free of dogmatism: "Mr. Franklin had not elaborated a general system of politics for himself; he would examine problems as the course of events or his foresight would present them to his mind, and he would solve them with principles he drew from a pure soul and a sound and shrewd mind."[52]

Not only did Franklin's character and principles, as portrayed in the *Eulogy*, embody an image of the typical American that had widespread currency among the intellectual elites of the end of the Old Regime, they also corresponded to Condorcet's notion of the ideal philosophe. Thus Franklin is compared to Voltaire for his role in fighting against religious fanaticism. His selfless patriotism is likened to that of Socrates. He is even deemed superior to Pythagoras in his work toward the moral improvement of humankind: "The Greek philosopher wanted, by force of habit, to substitute for natural feelings and impulsions the principles he thought necessary to inspire in men; the American philosopher only wished to refine, strengthen and channel the movements of nature. One had intended to enslave and transform man, the other only aspired to enlighten and improve him." Like the great sages of the past, Franklin had achieved mastery over the self and its passions: "He had invented for himself a method by which one could hope to improve oneself by means of a small number of rules the daily observation of which was meant to destroy imperceptibly those habits of weakness and passions that are detrimental to happiness and degrade morals, and then give wisdom and virtue all the strength of a natural inclination." But nature always remained his ultimate guide: "More than once in his works he took pleasure in setting the naïve good sense of the Indians against the proud reason of civilized men, and their unfailing calm and profound indifference, against the passions which trouble us for imaginary interests. He seemed to think that the savage was less different than most of us from what man perfected by reason, without ceasing to be subject to nature, would be."[53]

Perhaps the most important quality Condorcet associated with his picture of the ideal philosopher was dedication to public service and to the general improvement of society. This is the dimension of Franklin's life and career most emphasized in the *Eulogy*. As already mentioned, the first pages give a detailed description of Franklin's early inclination in this direction. He would soon confirm his civic-mindedness by founding several public institutions in Philadelphia, notably a library, a hospital, a college, and an academy. And later, of course, his public service would extend to his playing a pivotal role in shaping the destiny of his country.

Franklin's career in politics and diplomacy provided Condorcet with a welcome opportunity to revisit the American Revolution, including the historical events that led to it, particularly from the Seven Years' War on. Concerning the Revolution itself, he reiterates his previously expressed misgivings about the new Federal Constitution by presenting Franklin as having shared the same concerns. On the other hand, he praises the 1776 Pennsylvania constitution, of which Franklin had been one of the main architects, and adds some illuminating remarks on what he considered the conservative impulse behind bicameralism—a bicameral system tends to maintain the status quo and make reforms difficult:

> [The constitution of Pennsylvania] differs from most of the others by a greater equality, and from all, in that the legislative power is entrusted to a single chamber of representatives; Mr. Franklin's opinion alone determined this last provision. . . . Mr. Franklin was aware that the procedure for debate in a single assembly can procure everything needed to give its decisions the deliberate maturity which guarantees their truth and wisdom; whereas the establishment of two chambers leads to avoiding new mistakes only by perpetuating existing errors. The contrary opinion is due to that discouraging philosophy which regards error and corruption as the normal state of societies, and moments of virtue and reason as wonders one cannot hope to make last. It was time for both a nobler and truer philosophy to preside over the destiny of humankind, and Mr. Franklin was worthy of setting the first example thereof.[54]

No doubt in part because of the strong English influence reflected in the new Federal Constitution and the recent adoption of a new bicameral constitution by Pennsylvania in 1790, the *Eulogy* does not stress the novelty of the American example as emphatically as *Influence of the American Revolution on Europe* had done. Condorcet still contrasts the New World with the Old when he writes, "Men easily come to an agreement when a gentle equality has preserved them from the sophisms of interest and vanity; truth is easy to find for an emerging nation free of prejudices, and it is principally to counter the systematic errors of habit and corruption that old nations need all the resources of education, all the powers of genius." But he also mentions the important political role of English heritage in the formation of American liberty:

> Americans had always been free. They were governed by English laws, but these laws were those of their ancestors. They had not received

them, but they had brought them along with them; and yet, what is most contrary to civil liberty in these laws had been naturally eliminated, and Americans had been unwilling to tolerate either those remnants of feudalism, or those infringements upon the right to make free use of one's industry, which disgrace English legislation. Their charters protected them from all the violence of arbitrary power. No tax could be collected from them without their consent. Strict equality among men, and far greater religious freedom, made them in fact freer than the English. . . . Therefore, it was not for them a question of conquering their freedom, but of defending it, not of recovering rights that had been usurped from them, but of maintaining these rights.[55]

In relation to England, the American Revolution represents continuity and progress at the same time. The Americans gave English liberty a universal and truly democratic character.

Progress is the great theme of the concluding pages of the *Eulogy*. The figure of the scientist-philosopher-legislator embodied by Franklin, and also by Condorcet himself of course, marks the culmination of a long historical process begun during the Renaissance, when the invention of printing vastly expanded the diffusion of knowledge:

> The invention of printing had established rapid communication between nations where Latin was the common language of all educated men. They had ceased to be foreign to one another, and all men who could read had become fellow citizens. For a long time, religious quarrels were nearly the only fruit of this coming together; but when, through the progress of enlightenment, true science replaced systems, and a philosophy based on nature and observation supplanted the prejudices of the schools, enlightened men of all countries began to form only a single body, ruled by the same principles, and heading toward a single goal. Then, everywhere reason and freedom gained peaceful apostles, independent in their opinions, but united in their worship of these beneficent divinities.[56]

This last sentence points to a central notion in Condorcet's vision of progress: humankind has reached a stage in its history when reason and freedom, science and politics, or, as the academician would often put it, the physical and moral sciences, will necessarily experience parallel progress. He was convinced that the moral sciences could become as exact and rigorous in their description of phenomena as the physical.[57] Here, the author of the *Eulogy* projects himself so thoroughly onto his subject that he clearly attributes his own views to Franklin, describing him as "a man who knew that the moral world, like the physical world, is subject to fixed laws," and therefore could see "that the French Revolution, like the American, was one of those events which human reason can withdraw from the rule of chance and passions." Moreover, without the support of the sciences freedom can never be established on a firm basis, "for, in the natural order of things, political enlightenment follows in their wake, relies on their progress, or can only cast, as among the ancients, an uncertain, passing and troubled light." So the *Eulogy* concludes with a tribute to the political role of science, its fostering of independent and critical thinking: "Always free in the midst of all tyrannies, the sciences convey to those who study them something of their noble independence; either they flee from countries subjected to arbitrary power, or they gently prepare the revolution which is to destroy it; they form a large class of men used to thinking for themselves, to taking pleasure in the search for truth and in the approbation of their peers, too enlightened, in the end, to fail to know their rights, even when they are prudent enough to wait silently for the moment to recover them."[58] Such is the paramount lesson taught by Franklin's exemplary life: science and liberty always sustain one another, they are inseparable manifestations of the same process of human emancipation. A nation that fails to cultivate the sciences and promote education can never be truly free. Or, as Condorcet asserts in the very last words of the *Eulogy*, "even under the freest constitution, an ignorant people is always enslaved."[59]

Along with the chapters on the American Revolution in Raynal and Diderot's *History of the East and West Indies*, Condorcet's writings on the United States represent the most important political texts on the young republic to have been published by Americanist philosophes toward the end of the Old Regime. As Durand Echeverria points out in his exhaustive study on the image of America in France up to 1815, two different perspectives on American society prevailed among the liberal intellectual elites of prerevolutionary France.[60] Both interpretations associated the United States with notions of liberty and enlightenment, but one favored images of virtue and simplicity, whereas the other emphasized the idea of progress.[61] The *History of the East and West Indies* shows more affinity with the "virtue and simplicity" paradigm. Raynal and Diderot tend to see America as a recreation of an ideal past of equality and frugality, much in the spirit of the republicanism of antiquity. Condorcet, on the other hand, offers probably the best example of the "progress" paradigm. His vision of America insists on new, modern constructions of freedom, and on the potential for future advances in science, industry, and global trade. Thus Condorcet's reflections on the United States hold a privileged place in both his political writings and the history of the French Revolution. They helped him elaborate a constitutional model inspired by the early American Revolution, one that was resolutely forward-looking, progressive, and anchored in modernity. Based on the recognition of natural rights and on institutions meant to foster enlightened, open debate and rational, collective decision making, this model is of crucial importance insofar as it became one of the three great sources of constitutional inspiration available to the French revolutionaries—the other two being Montesquieu's distillation, in *The Spirit of the Laws*, of the essence of the government of England (i.e., the system of separation and balance of powers, with two legislative chambers embodying different interests),[62] and Rousseau's reformulation of ancient communitarian republicanism in *Du contrat social* (1762) (*The Social Contract*).

As the *Eulogy of Franklin* shows, Condorcet remained an américaniste to the end. He was well aware that the Federal Constitution was the product of an unavoidable struggle between universal principles of freedom and justice on one hand, and local factors or leftover prejudice on the other. Compromises had to be made; sometimes old prejudices prevailed, most notably in the case of slavery. But he firmly believed that, with time, universal principles would win out. And to some extent, he was right, although not on the point that was for him the most important: America never returned to the unicameral system Condorcet had admired in Pennsylvania's first constitution and in the Articles of Confederation, a system that the French Revolution, in contrast, adopted. On the other hand, a declaration of rights was quickly added to the Constitution, jury trial was extended to civil cases,[63] slavery was eventually abolished,[64] senators are no longer elected by the legislatures of the states but, like members of the House of Representatives, by direct popular vote,[65] and presidents are now limited to two terms.[66]

Condorcet remained fundamentally optimistic about the prospects opened up by the revolution in America, just as later, even when it was his turn to be branded as counterrevolutionary, even in the face of persecution by the Jacobins, he continued to believe in the righteousness of the revolution in

France. By June 1793, the French Revolution had moved away from liberal constitutionalism and toward a regime based on terror and the exploitation of movements of popular insurrection, an evolution that Condorcet could only oppose, attached as he was to individual liberties and the rule of law. He issued a written protest against the hurried imposition of a Jacobin constitution,[67] the Convention called for his arrest on July 8, and he was forced into hiding. Thus the progressive constitutionalist fell victim to the radical, terrorist politics of the Jacobins. Nevertheless, in his last and most famous work, the posthumous *Esquisse d'un tableau historique des progrès de l'esprit humain* (1795) (Outline of a historical chart of the progress of the human mind), written while hiding from the Terror during the last few months before his arrest and death in prison in March 1794, Condorcet criticized the American revolutionaries for having, unlike the French, too often substituted "identity of interests" for the principle of equality of rights.[68] Persecution and tyranny had not shaken his faith in the principles of the French Revolution. Similarly, despite his reservations concerning the Federal Constitution, he also retained his confidence in the young American republic's ability to realize with time the full promise of its democratic ideals: "[One of these revolutions (the French Revolution)] would be swifter and more thorough, but more violent; [the other (the American Revolution)] would be less swift and less thorough, but also less violent[; in the first,] freedom and happiness would be purchased at the price of transient evils; [in the other,] these evils would be avoided but, it might be, at the price of long delaying the harvest of [some of] the fruits *that the revolution must, nevertheless, inevitably bear.*"[69] Having embraced history as the gradual deployment of reason—in the sphere of knowledge as well as in the domain of social organization—Condorcet's fundamental optimism did not have to rest on the immediate success of any particular revolution; rather, he could place his hopes in the human capacity to overcome obstacles in the long, indeed virtually endless, (r)evolutionary process/progress toward a free and rational society.

Influence of the American Revolution on Europe (1786)

To the Marquis de Lafayette,[1]
Who, at an age when ordinary men are barely known in their
own country, has deserved the title of Benefactor of two Worlds.

By an obscure inhabitant of the old hemisphere.

Introduction

The path of truth, said the poet Saadi,[2] is narrow and lies between two preci-
pices. At the slightest misstep, one tumbles to the bottom. One picks oneself
up, dazed by the fall, struggles back toward the top, believes it is within
reach, makes a last effort, and falls again on the other side.

No sooner had America declared its independence than our politicians
saw clearly that the ruin of England and the prosperity of France had to be
the necessary consequence of this happy revolution. Now that this independence is recognized and assured, they seem to consider it with indifference,
and only at the time when events are beginning to validate the latter part of
their predictions do they decide to entertain doubts about them.

I believe that this moment when public opinion appears to err in an opposite direction, is precisely the time when it can be useful to discuss calmly
the consequences of this great event, and I will try to be a prophet without
passion.

The prize proposed by the Abbé Raynal,[3] on the good or harm that the
discovery of the New World has done to Europe, had aroused my interest;
I had dared to undertake to solve this problem, but I realized that the task
was beyond my powers, and I have saved from the flames only the chapter
where I examined the influence that America's independence would have
on humankind, on Europe, on France in particular, and also the analysis of
certain principles according to which I tried to find a method of measuring
the different levels of public happiness.

Since a nation taken as a whole is an abstract being, it can be neither
happy nor unhappy. Thus, when one speaks of the collective happiness of a
nation, one can mean only two things, either a kind of mean value resulting

from the happiness and unhappiness of individuals, or the general means that can contribute to happiness, that is to say, to the peace and welfare that the land, the laws, industry, relations with foreign nations can provide to the citizenry in general. A simple sense of justice is enough to realize that only the latter meaning need be considered.

Otherwise, it would be necessary to adopt the maxim, all too common among republicans ancient and modern, that the smaller number can be legitimately sacrificed to the greater, a maxim which places society in a state of perpetual war and subjects to the rule of force what should only be ruled by reason and justice.[4]

For man as a social being, the general means leading to happiness can be divided into two classes. The first includes everything that secures and extends the free enjoyment of his natural rights. The second contains the means of diminishing the number of ills to which nature has subjected humankind, of satisfying our basic needs more surely and with less labor, of providing greater comfort to ourselves by the exercise of our powers and the legitimate use of our industries. Consequently, the means through which we can enhance our strength and industry must be included in this same class.

The rights of man are:

1. The security of his person, which includes the assurance not to be disturbed by any violence, either within his household or in the use of his faculties, the free and independent exercise of which he must retain in everything not contrary to the rights of another.

2. The security and free enjoyment of his property.

3. Since in society there are certain actions which must be regulated by common rules, since penalties must be established for infringements by an individual, either by violence or fraud, on the rights of another, man also has the right to be subjected in all these matters only to general laws extending to the entire citizenry, the interpretation of which cannot be arbitrary and the execution of which is entrusted to impartial hands.

4. Finally, the right to contribute, either directly or through representatives, to the making of these laws and to every act carried out in the name of society follows necessarily from the natural and primitive equality of man, and an equal enjoyment of this right by each man with the use of his reason must be regarded as the ultimate goal we must strive to reach. As long as it has not been attained, it cannot be said that citizens enjoy this final right to its full extent.[5]

There is not one among the rights of men that cannot be easily derived from those to which we have just tried to reduce them, and it would even be easy to prove that all the principles of civil and criminal law, as well as those of laws regarding administration, trade, or police, are consequences of the obligation to respect the rights included under the first three headings.

The happiness of a society is greater, the more extensively these rights belong to the members of the state. But the enjoyment of each of these same rights is not equally important for public happiness; we have listed them here in the order in which we believe them to contribute to this happiness, and we will even add that in a very populous society it must almost necessarily happen that the last of these rights turns out to be nearly nonexistent for the majority of the inhabitants of a country.

Some zealous republicans have regarded it as the most important of all, and to be sure, in an enlightened nation free of all superstition, where it would really belong to every citizen who could or would exercise it, the enjoyment of this right would ensure that of all the others. But it loses its most precious value, if ignorance and prejudice lead those who are to exercise it away from the narrow path traced for them by the immutable laws of justice, and with respect to public happiness, a republic with tyrannical laws can be far inferior to a monarchy.[6]

In adopting this order, it remains clear that the very frequent or very serious violation of a less essential right can be more harmful to public happiness than the minor or very rare violation of a more important right. Thus, for example, a procedure in criminal jurisprudence which would expose innocent people to conviction by ignorant or partial judges can do more harm to a country than a law which would apply the death penalty to an imaginary crime very rare where this punishment is established. Tax laws, restrictive trade laws can, by undermining the free enjoyment of property, be more harmful than an arbitrary power of imprisonment that would only be used very rarely.

These principles are simple, but evaluating the degrees of harm or good that can result from these various infringements on natural rights, or from the elimination of abuses contrary to these rights, becomes a difficult task. It would not be enough to know with precision the effects of each unjust law, of each useful reform, it would also be necessary to have a common measure to which these effects could be compared.

As for the second class of means conducive to happiness, it is easy to see that they also depend in very large part on the freer and more extensive exercise of natural rights. Beyond this, they simply consist, first in the enjoyment of a secure and durable peace with foreign powers, then in multiplying the means to procure for ourselves more comfort with equal labor, either by increasing knowledge and industry, or by extending relations with other peoples, or, more importantly, by a greater equality in the distribution of these means among members of society. Indeed, since population is necessarily proportional to the means of subsistence produced during a normal year, it is clear that, for the majority of citizens, the quantity of goods to be enjoyed can never be very great, at least in any constant and lasting way. Therefore, it is in the more equitable distribution of these goods that one must seek public happiness, and all civil laws, all laws relating to trade must tend to maintain or restore this equality among members of a nation, without interfering with the right of property or the legitimate exercise of freedom.[7]

It follows from these same principles that the happiness of a people, far from increasing with the misfortune or weakness of its neighbors, must on the contrary grow with the prosperity of other peoples, since it would then receive from them the example of good laws, of the elimination of abuses, of new methods of industry, all the advantages, in short, resulting from the communication of knowledge and enlightenment. And it is clear at the same time that the amount of goods to be enjoyed in common and the ability to distribute them more equally are for all peoples the necessary effect of the progress of each.

The only exception to this general rule is the case when a people, led astray by a misguided policy, wearies its neighbors with its ambition and attempts at its own expense, either through war, monopolies or restrictive trade laws, to make its power dangerous and its prosperity useless to them.

Such are the principles according to which I will try to show what the influence of the American Revolution must be.

Perhaps the author of these reflections will be credited with no achievement other than dreaming on a larger scale than the Abbé de Saint-Pierre,[8] and he will reply in the same way: I will easily console myself for having been considered a dreamer all my life, if I can hope that a century after me the realization of one of my ideas might do a little good.

This is even too much to ask. In seeking to spread some isolated truths sterile in themselves, one can in the long run facilitate more felicitous and fruitful combinations of ideas. Is it not also useful to help draw the attention of good minds to an important matter and inspire them with the desire to make it the object of their meditations or investigations? One would not be entitled to the glory they might deserve, but could at least claim some right to the pleasure of having occasioned some good. And would it be paying too dearly for this pleasure to purchase it with a small sacrifice of one's pride and with the embarrassment of having been mistaken in good faith, or of having pronounced only minor and common truths on great matters?

Chapter One

Influence of the American Revolution on the Opinions and Legislation of Europe

"Humankind had lost its rights, Montesquieu recovered them and gave them back to us."[i] But it is not enough for these rights to be written in the books of philosophers and in the hearts of virtuous men, ignorant or weak men must be able to read them in the example of a great people.

America has given us this example. Its Declaration of Independence is a simple and sublime exposition of these rights, so sacred and so long forgotten. No nation has known them so well or preserved them with such perfect integrity.

It is true, negroes are still enslaved in some of the United States, but all enlightened men feel the shame, as well as the danger, of slavery, and soon this blemish will no longer sully the purity of American laws.[9]

These wise republicans, still attached to some remains of English prejudices, have not sufficiently recognized that restrictive laws, trade regulations, and indirect taxes were real infringements on the right of property, of which these practices limit the free exercise, for one does not own what one cannot dispose of.[10] While instituting a more extensive tolerance than any other nation, they consented to some limitations demanded by the people but contrary, if not to the exercise of personal freedom, at least to the right of each man not to incur any penalty for believing what his reason has commanded him to believe. Perhaps it would also be possible to find in the laws of some states slight remnants of a fanaticism too soured by long persecutions to yield to the first efforts of philosophy; but if these infringements on the natural rights of men are compared with all those an enlightened observer could

i. Voltaire.

discover in the legislations of the wisest peoples, above all those ancient nations that are so admired and so little known, it will become clear that our opinion of American laws is not the result of an exaggerated enthusiasm, either for that nation or for our own century.

Besides, if the Americans can be justly criticized, it is only for individual errors or old abuses that circumstances have not allowed them to correct. They will only need to be consistent to rectify them all. Unlike every other nation so far, one finds among them neither Machiavellian maxims elevated to the status of political principles, nor, among the leaders, the sincere or feigned opinion that it is impossible to improve the social order and to reconcile public prosperity with justice.

The example of a great people among whom the rights of man are respected is useful to all others despite differences in climate, manners, and constitutions. It shows that these rights are everywhere the same and that except for one,[11] which, under some constitutions, virtuous citizens must renounce in the interest of public tranquility, there is no country where man cannot enjoy all his other rights to their full extent.

Such an example makes apparent the influence of the enjoyment of these rights on public prosperity, by showing that men who have never feared insults against their person acquire a gentler and more elevated soul, that he whose property is always secure finds it easy to be honest, that citizens who are ruled only by the laws have more patriotism and courage.

This example, so useful to all the nations that can observe it, was about to be lost to the human race. Great nations look down upon the example of small ones, and England, which for a century had provided such an imposing one, was only going to lend credence by its fall to the all too common, too dangerous and too erroneous opinion that laws can only temporarily hold sway over peoples and that political bodies are doomed to dissolve themselves after a few moments of more or less brilliant life.[12] If America had succumbed to England's weapons, soon despotism would have forged there the shackles of the mother country, and the English would have experienced the fate of all the republics that have ceased to be free because they wanted to have subjects instead of simply citizens.[13]

England would have lost its laws in losing its liberty. No doubt, it can happen that in a peaceful monarchy a wise legislator is respectful enough of human rights to make proud republicans envy the lot of its happy subjects. We know that this truth, important for the stability of these constitutions, was demonstrated by some French philosophers,[14] at the very time when they were being accused in newspapers, government orders and court indictments, of preaching sedition. But violence alone can subjugate those who have once enjoyed freedom; and for citizens to consent to cease to be free, they must be deprived even of their human dignity.

As a necessary consequence of the respect of American laws for the natural rights of humankind, any man, whatever his religion, opinions or principles, is sure to find asylum there. In vain did England offer the same opportunity, at least to Protestants. The industriousness of its inhabitants leaves no avenue for that of foreigners, its wealth turns away the poor, there is little room left in a land where trade and manufacturing have multiplied the population. Even its climate is suited only to a small part of the peoples of Europe. America, on the other hand, offers attractive hopes to industry, there a poor man can easily earn his keep, and a secure property, sufficient to satisfy his needs, can become the fruit of his labor. A more varied climate can suit men from every country.

At the same time, America is separated from the peoples of Europe by a vast expanse of ocean. To be prompted to cross it, motives other than a simple desire to improve one's well-being are needed. Only the oppressed can wish to surmount such an obstacle. Thus, without having to fear mass emigration, Europe finds in America a useful restraint on ministers who could be tempted to misgovern. Oppression must become more timid in Europe when it recognizes that an asylum remains to those it would have marked out as its victims, and that they can both escape and punish it by forcing it to appear with them before the court of public opinion.

Freedom of the press is established in America, and there the right to say and hear truths that are considered useful has been regarded with just reason as one of the most sacred rights of humankind.

In a country where the willow is a sacred tree and where it would be forbidden, under penalty of death, to break off one of its branches to save a drowning man, could it be said that the law does not infringe at all upon the freedom or security of citizens? If the absurdity of laws against freedom of the press does not appear as palpable to us, it is because, unfortunately, habit has the sinister power to accustom our feeble human reason to what should revolt it most.

The mere example of all the good that freedom of the press has done and will continue to do in America will be all the more useful to Europe since it is better suited than that of England to reassure against the alleged dangers of this freedom. More than once already, we have seen Americans comply peacefully with laws the principles or consequences of which they had force-fully attacked, and respectfully obey the representatives of public authority, without giving up the right to try to enlighten them and to point out to the nation their failures or their mistakes. We have witnessed public discussions dispel prejudices and prepare the widespread support of public opinion for the wise views of these burgeoning legislations.

We have seen freedom of the press, far from facilitating intrigue, disband private associations and prevent those led by personal designs from forming factions, and we have been able to conclude that harangues and libels are dangerous only insofar as severe laws force them to circulate clandestinely.

Finally, we have seen in America that information, easily and quickly disseminated throughout an immense country by way of the printing press, gave the government, in difficult circumstances, a weapon often more pow-erful than the laws. Of this, we will mention only one example: desertion had found its way into part of the militia, the most severe penalties could not stop it because the hope of impunity stripped them of all their force. It was proposed that the name of the guilty be published in their local gazette, and the fear of this punishment was more efficient than the fear of death. One understands that such a noble and generous way of calling citizens back to their duty owes all its success to the right of the accused to protest, with equal publicity, against a false accusation.

In England, the practice of circumventing, by often ridiculous subtleties, the remaining laws against freedom of the press, the scandal of libels, the ve-nality of political writers, the false ardor of a patriotism that is not genuinely felt, have all prevented notice of the fact that the country owes to the freedom of the press even more than to its constitution the stability of its laws and its continued respect for those human rights sanctioned by public opinion.[15]

Can we believe that governments of countries where intolerance still reigns, when they see that the most extensive tolerance ever enjoyed by any people, far from inciting unrest, is making peace and fraternity flourish in America, will continue to consider intolerance necessary to the tranquility of the state and not learn at last that they can without danger obey the voice of justice and humanity? In the past, fanaticism dared show itself openly and ask for men's blood in the name of God; reason has forced it into hiding; it has put on the mask of politics and it is for the sake of peace that it asks still to be left with the means to disturb it. But America has proved that a coun-try can be happy without persecutors or hypocrites in its midst, and politi-cians who would have found it difficult to believe this on the authority of philosophers, will doubtless believe it on account of this example.[16]

In observing how the Americans have based their peace and happiness on a small number of maxims which seem a candid expression of what common sense could have dictated to all men, we will stop praising these exceedingly complex mechanisms in which a multitude of parts leads to a forced, irregular and difficult operation, and so many counterweights that are said to balance each other out join together in reality to weigh down on the people. Perhaps we will perceive the futility, or rather the danger of these political subtleties that have been admired for too long, these systems designed to force the laws, and consequently truth, reason and justice, their immutable foundations, to change according to the temperature, to conform to the types of government, to the practices sanctioned by prejudice, and even to the follies adopted by each people, as if it would not have been more human, just and noble to seek in a rational legislation the means of disabusing peoples with regard to their errors.[17]

We will see that it is possible to have brave warriors, obedient soldiers and disciplined troops without recourse to the harshness of military administrations in several nations in Europe, where the lower ranks are judged on the basis of secret reports by their commanders, convicted without being heard, punished without being able to defend themselves, where it is a new crime to ask to prove one's innocence and a much greater crime still to declare in print that one is not guilty. It must be admitted, however, that neither corruption, nor deliberate injustice, nor tyrannical cruelty should be held responsible for this system of secret oppression which violates the rights of both citizens and nations; still less should it be attributed to necessity for it is at the same time as useless and as dangerous to discipline and the security of the state as it can be unjust. What then is to blame? Alas! Only our insurmountable ignorance of natural law can excuse this sin, and the example of a people who are free and yet peacefully complying with military as well as civil laws will no doubt have the power to cure us.

The example of the equality which exists in the United States and ensures its peace and prosperity can also be useful to Europe. To be sure, we no longer believe here that nature has divided the human race, like horses, into three or four categories, and that one of these categories is also doomed to work much and eat little. We have been told so much about the benefits of business and trade that a nobleman is now beginning to look upon a banker and a merchant, as long as they are very rich, almost as his equals. But our philosophy goes no further, and not long ago we still argued in print that in certain countries the common people are by nature subject to the taille and to unpaid forced labor.[18]

We said, not so long ago, that the sense of honor can fully exist only in certain social classes and that it was necessary to degrade the greater part of a nation in order to give the rest a little more pride.[19]

But here is what one will be able to read in America's history. A young French general,[20] whose mission was to defend Virginia against a stronger army, seeing that soldiers who had been taken from their regiments to form his body of troops were abandoning it, declared, in order to stop this sort of desertion, that since he wished to have with him select men, he would send back to the army everyone whose courage, loyalty or intelligence he viewed with suspicion. From that moment on no one considered leaving. A soldier the general wanted to entrust with a particular mission made him promise that if he happened to die on his mission his local gazette would publish that he had left the detachment on the general's orders only. Another soldier, unable to walk because of an injury, rented a wagon at his own expense to keep up with the army. Such anecdotes will compel us to admit that the sense of honor is the same under all constitutions, that it is felt with equal force by men of all conditions, provided that no social class is degraded by an unjust opinion or oppressed by bad laws.

Such are the benefits humankind as a whole should expect from America's example, and we would be surprised if these benefits were regarded as illusory because they do not have an immediate and physical influence on the lot of individuals. This would be to ignore the fact that the happiness of men assembled in society depends almost entirely on good laws, and that if men owe their first tribute to the legislator who combines the wisdom to conceive them with the will and power to prescribe them, those who, by their example or their lessons, show each legislator the laws he should make, become after him the greatest benefactors of peoples.

Chapter Two

On the Benefits of the American Revolution with Respect to
the Preservation of Peace in Europe

The Abbé de Saint-Pierre had dared to believe that one day men would be reasonable enough for nations to consent by common agreement to forego the barbaric right to wage war and refer the discussion of their claims, interests or grievances to the judgment of peaceful mediators. Undoubtedly, this is not purely a visionary idea; it is so clearly demonstrated that war can never be to the benefit of the majority of individuals in a nation! Why should men, who for so long have agreed to indulge in absurd and fatal errors, not concur one day to adopt simple and beneficial truths? But this hope is still far from becoming a reality.

Perhaps the Abbé de Saint-Pierre would have been more helpful if instead of recommending that sovereigns (monarchs, senates or peoples) forego the right to wage war, he had proposed that they retain this right but at the same time institute a court responsible for judging, on behalf of all nations, disputes that may arise between them concerning the handing over of criminals, the application of trade laws, the seizure of foreign ships, violations of borders, the interpretation of treaties, rights of succession, etc. The various states would have reserved the right to implement the decisions of the court or appeal to the judgment of force. Members of this tribunal would have been instructed to draw up a code of international law, based exclusively on reason and justice, which federated nations would have agreed to observe in times of peace. They would have written another code meant to contain rules that it would be in the general interest to observe in times of war, either between warring nations or between them and neutral powers. By creating more union between peoples in peacetime, such a tribunal could smother the seeds of war and destroy the germs of hatred as well as the kind of animosity of one people towards another which predisposes nations to war and causes them to seize on every pretext for it. Often, ambitious men who advocate war would not dare propose it without flattering themselves that they can rouse popular opinion in their favor—without the support of the very people whose blood and means of subsistence they squander. Wars would become less cruel. Indeed, we are still very far from giving justice and humanity everything they can be granted in wartime without jeopardizing the chance for victory. Regular armies have at least produced one great benefit: making populations alien to the war waged in their name; and there is no reason why an enemy should not treat the inhabitants of a borderland he has conquered as he would those of his own if he had to defend it. Is it so necessary to the success of naval wars to legitimate theft and plunder? Have we even pondered with any attention the sad benefits and fatal consequences of this practice inherited from barbaric centuries and nations? But let us not stray from our topic with these ideas which, as simple and natural as they may be to any man endowed with a just heart and a sound mind, would still stun the ears of politicians.

Let us come to the effects of the American Revolution and see whether, although it has cost humankind a war, it has not been beneficial even in this respect.

If England and its colonies had made their peace, the British ministry would have perceived that a foreign war was the only way to extract taxes from them, to establish military authority there and gain political support. This war with the House of Bourbon would have led to the loss of many islands in the West Indies, which France and Spain could not have defended against America and England together. In itself, I would not consider the loss of the sugar islands as a very great misfortune for France. Subtracting the costs of cultivation, administration and defense, the product of these islands adds only a very small amount to the total product of France's territory, and these possessions that are so difficult to defend diminish rather than increase the power of the nation. The situation would be different, however, if it were feared that a nation, ill informed on the real interests of its own trade, might grant rich and greedy merchants a monopoly over foreign trade, a monopoly the weight of which that nation itself and in particular less wealthy merchants would also feel. In this case, the interest of each consumer nation would be to secure the means of providing for itself, at least in part, commodities that have become necessary, without being subject to the whims of other nations. From this point of view, the possession of colonies in the West Indies is truly important for European nations.

The general principles of political economy have been rigorously demonstrated, they admit no real exceptions. If they cannot be followed in practice, if their consequences cannot be extended to every particular case, it is only because many men allow themselves to be guided by prejudices contrary to these principles; thus, these apparent exceptions only confirm them further. In the case we are considering, the loss of the sugar islands would have had disastrous consequences for France. The French navy, destroyed in an ill-fated war, would have left England master of the seas. Soon it would have wanted to seize control of the commerce of India, Africa, and of both North and South America.

The monopolistic spirit of its trade policies would have prompted England to take the measures most ruinous to other nations, even at the expense of its own wealth, and would have exposed them to every vexation and insult a mercantilist policy can conceive. But into how many wars would the nations of Europe have been dragged before this Machiavellian system had run its course and the British Empire collapsed? For this system would have been unevenly but continuously followed by ministers in whose interest it would have been to keep their nation occupied with conquests, either to stay in power, avoid domestic unrest or the independence of the colonies, or undermine the constitution and give rise to an absolute monarchy. Perhaps more than a century of oppression and warfare would have elapsed before the breakup of that empire would bring back peace and freedom on the seas. Thus, humankind can forgive the American revolutionary war on account of the ills which that war averted.

The same revolution will make warfare rarer in Europe.

Indeed, there is no escaping the fact that in the West Indies the Americans are almost entirely free to tip the scale in favor of whichever European power they support. At the same time, they can conquer and keep their conquests there more easily than European nations. Moreover, the inhabitants of these islands are rather indifferent to the name of the power that governs them because they are more like manufacturers than genuine owners attached to the land. They would be inclined to join with a people who does not deign to rule over subjects, who wants to have fellow citizens only, and for whom to conquer can only mean to let the conquered share in their independence and liberty. To be sure, if the Americans abolish negro slavery in their country and European powers are barbaric enough to follow the pernicious policy of maintaining it, English, French or Spanish colonists may fear, more than desire, the arrival of Americans in their possessions. But then the Americans would only be more assured of their success since they would have, upon arriving on each island, numerous supporters motivated by all the courage that vengeance and the hope of freedom can inspire.

Thus, as soon as the United States have repaired the damage which was the price of their independence, no European nation will be able to undertake, without imprudence, a war in seas where it would be at risk of losing everything if it had the United States as enemies, or becoming their dependent if it had them as friends.

Very soon, perhaps as early as today had the American Revolution not taken place, the possession of the West Indies would have been extremely precarious; it will doubtless become so, but later. Besides, the English would certainly have considered the conquest of these islands very important, and the Americans are unlikely ever to have the same idea. They realize that it is essential to their freedom and the preservation of their rights not to have subjects; they cannot wish to have weak allies far away from them who are difficult to defend; and Europeans alone, by an imprudent course of action, could prompt them to undertake such a conquest. The French ministry recognized this and if it hastened to open its colonies to the Americans,[21] this measure, just in itself, necessary to the prosperity and almost the existence of the colonies, was at the same time dictated by a wise and farsighted policy.

Americans will also contribute to the preservation of peace in Europe through the influence of their example. In the Old World, some eloquent philosophers, above all Voltaire, have protested against the injustice and absurdity of war, but they have only been able to soften in some respects the warlike furor which reigns in Europe. The vast number of men who can only expect glory and fortune from the massacre of their fellows have insulted their zeal, and it was repeated in books, in military camps and in courts, that patriotism and virtue had vanished ever since an abominable philosophy had decided to spare human blood.

But in America, these same peaceful opinions are those of a great people, a courageous people who have proved capable of defending their homes and breaking their chains. There, any idea of war undertaken because of ambition or a desire for conquest is condemned by the calm judgment of a humane and peaceful nation. There, the language of humanity and justice cannot be ridiculed either by the warmongering courtiers of a king or the ambitious leaders of a republic. There, the honor of defending the homeland is the greatest of all, without the military profession weighing down pridefully upon the citizenry. What will the militaristic prejudices of Europe be able to offer to refute this example?

Chapter Three

Benefits of the American Revolution with Respect to
the Perfectibility of the Human Race

We have already tried to show to what extent the American example and the knowledge that will result from the freedom to discuss every question important to men's happiness can be instrumental in the destruction of prejudices still existing in Europe. But there is another sort of benefit on which we believe we must pause, even though we are quite convinced that it will seem illusory to the majority of our readers.

America presents a country of vast dimensions where several million men live whose education has preserved them from prejudice and inclined toward study and reflection. No social distinctions exist there, no rewards for ambition which could lure these men away from the natural desire to perfect their minds, to engage in useful investigations and to aspire to the glory attached to great works or discoveries; and nothing there confines a part of the human race to a state of abjection where it is doomed to stupidity and misery. Therefore, there is reason to hope that a few generations from now, America, by producing almost as many men who will be busy adding to the extent of our knowledge as all of Europe, will at least double its progress or make it twice as fast. Such progress will include the useful arts as well as the speculative sciences.

The benefits humankind can gain thereby must be counted among the effects of the American Revolution. To be sure, dependence on the mother country would not have extinguished the natural genius of Americans, and Mr. Franklin is proof of this. But almost always, it would have diverted this genius toward other objects. The desire to be somebody in England would have smothered every other sentiment in the soul of an American born with energy and talents, and he would have chosen the fastest and surest ways to achieve this goal. Those who could not have entertained such ambition would have fallen into despondency and indolence.

States ruled by princes who govern from far away, provinces too distant from the capitals of great empires provide us with striking proofs of this assertion, and we would develop them here if not for the fear of appearing to pose as judges of genius and appraisers of nations and discoveries.

The reader will be surprised, perhaps, to see me place here a few discoveries or inventions and the progress of our knowledge, on a par with such great matters as the protection of human rights and the preservation of peace, and even ahead of benefits that can result from trade.

But having long reflected upon the ways to improve the fate of humankind, I cannot help but think that there is really only one: accelerating the progress of enlightenment. Any other means has only a passing and limited effect. Even if we admitted that errors, fables, and legislations put together according to local prejudices instead of reason, have made some nations happy, we would also be obliged to admit that everywhere this overly praised happiness has vanished quickly, to be replaced by evils which reason has still not been able to cure after several centuries.[22] Let men be enlightened, and soon you will see the good emerge effortlessly from the common will.[23]

Chapter Four

On the Good That the American Revolution Can Do,
Through Trade, to Europe and to France in Particular

So far, we have considered almost exclusively benefits which by their nature
are common to all countries. The preservation of peace is somewhat more
important to nations such as France, Spain, England and Holland, which are
at risk of war in the West Indies.

Likewise, France will benefit more than any other people in Europe
from the sound ideas of Americans on property rights and natural freedom,
because, with a greater need for these ideas than England, it has reached that
level of enlightenment allowing a nation to benefit from them and enjoys a
constitution under which useful reforms would find only a few obstacles to
surmount, and above all far fewer than in England.

Here again we will begin by examining the benefits that will result from
the American Revolution for the commerce of all nations; we will then see
whether France may enjoy some superiority in this respect. But before we
devote ourselves to this inquiry, it is useful to ask what sorts of benefits a
nation can find in foreign trade.

Through foreign trade, a nation can:

1. Obtain necessary or basic commodities that it lacks, obtain them at a
better price, and finally be more certain to have a dependable supply of them.

2. By increasing sales of domestic commodities or manufactured products, incite farmers to produce more and at the same time stimulate the industry and activity of manufacturers, which cannot grow without impacting
the size of the net product of the land and therefore real wealth.[24]

These two benefits, a more advantageous or reliable importation of commodities and new avenues for exports, may seem to be one and the same
since one can hardly exist without the other. But we make a distinction
between them because the direct purpose of the first is to improve the well-
being of the population and that of the second to generate more wealth.
Furthermore, it must be observed that production in a country cannot increase due to export sales without there resulting from this oversupply of
commodities a lesser risk of shortages.

One can also count among the benefits of foreign trade those that a nation
derives from its industriousness and trading skills. Thus, if a people lived on
a mere rock and had some capital, it could survive and even increase its

capital by receiving each year in return for its labor or trade speculations a portion of the income another nation draws from its land.

This third benefit, the greatest of all for a small people devoted exclusively to trade and industry, is almost inexistent for large nations occupying a vast territory.

Trade always consists of an exchange, and an exchange of materials that are renewed each year; otherwise it could not be sustained since a people who would trade every year a commodity that is not renewable for a commodity it needs would find itself unable to continue the exchange after a time.

But the method of exchange is not without importance:

1. Suppose that a country without rich mines buys, with silver, goods from another country. It is clear that it must have sold goods for silver to a third country. Thus, to perform what is really an exchange of goods for goods, the profit going to the merchant had to be paid twice. It would be paid only once if the exchange were direct, or in other words, a merchant who earns a profit from what he buys and sells can be satisfied with a smaller gain. Here is a savings in unnecessary costs for the population in general. It is not immaterial, then, whether identical goods are purchased with other goods or with silver, and everything else being equal, it is more advantageous to pay for them with goods.[25]

2. It is more beneficial to a country to export commodities the production of which requires more initial investment in proportion to the net profit, and is more variable and subject to accidents or weather conditions. Foreign trade is a way to find markets for these commodities during years of plenty and to make the livelihood of farmers less precarious. Thus, for example, it is preferable to export wine rather than wheat, wood, etc.

3. It is more advantageous to export manufactured products than commodities, because, as long as freedom of trade remains unlimited, agriculture receives the same stimulus from either. In one case farming is used to buy foreign goods, in the other to feed workers within the nation, and the effect is the same if agriculture is not impeded by restrictive laws. But in the first case agriculture alone is encouraged, in the second industry too, with the additional benefit of getting manufactured products of higher quality for the same price.

Finally, it is preferable, for the same reason, to import commodities rather than manufactured products, as long as the same condition of unlimited freedom of trade still applies. This condition is necessary because without it either the selling price of commodities will be lower or the purchase price of manufactured products will be higher, which will result in a real loss and may even cancel the benefits that can be expected from such a trade pattern.

Having established these principles, let us examine the benefits of a direct and expanded trade with America for Europe and for France.

First, any extension of free trade is a good thing:

1. Inasmuch as it necessarily creates more stimulus for agriculture on one hand, and a greater supply of goods to be enjoyed for the same price on the other.

2. Inasmuch as it will naturally and more quickly lead each country to grow and manufacture only what it can grow and manufacture most profitably. The increase in wealth and well-being which can result from reaching this natural order of things is immeasurable. Unfortunately, the sort of furor with which all nations want to grow and manufacture everything, not in order to perform simple experiments but so as to buy nothing from abroad, proves how much this benefit of free and extensive trade is ignored even today.

Aside from this benefit, since Americans occupy an immense territory a part of which has not yet been cleared for farming, they will for a long time remain a nation of farmers. In a free country, every man, whatever his industriousness, will necessarily prefer the condition of property owner to any other, as long as he can hope to become one without sacrificing too much of his well-being. Thus, for a long time to come, America will in general have only commodities to bring to Europe and manufactured products to ask for. It will have little silver to use in international trade because most of its capital will go into financing the clearing of land or settlements in remote regions. Therefore, it will only trade with Europe by direct exchanges of goods. Finally, the only commodity it will import from Europe, and for a long time to come, is wine, one of the most profitable to export.

At the same time, France seems to be the European nation for which trade with America is most important:

1. Because it has to use silver to buy from northern Europe oils, iron, hemp or wood it could obtain from America in exchange for manufactured products.

2. Because during years of shortage in wheat, wheat and rice from America would constitute an important resource for its provinces bordering the ocean or linked to it by canals and navigable rivers.

3. Because it can set up a very large trade in wine with America. And since France has a near monopoly over this particular trade and at the same

time can at least compete with England in manufacturing, it must naturally, thanks to the indispensible wine trade, be given preference over England in all others. And it will surely enjoy the same preference over the rest of European nations, so long as industry in Portugal and Spain does not experience progress.

It could be thought that on the contrary England would be preferred, and certainly, everything else being equal, the conformity of language, manners and religion, combined with habitual use of English manufactured products, could exert a great influence. But this influence, it must be observed, would be felt with all its force only initially; and at this early stage, remnants of an all too justified indignation as well as relations established during the recent war must necessarily diminish the effect of motives that could have induced the Americans to give preference to England, and France will have time to use means at its disposal to prevent such motives from counterbalancing its real advantages. Our factories will soon be able to conform to American tastes and needs, which our merchants will learn to know and anticipate.

Communication between the two peoples speaking different languages can be facilitated by setting up colleges in some of our cities, where Americans would send their children to be educated, where they would even send them in large numbers if all religious teaching were excluded.

Religion will not long remain an obstacle. The dogma dearest to Americans, the one they value most, is the dogma of religious tolerance or rather religious freedom, for among this people, governed more than any other by reason alone, the word "tolerance" seems almost an insult to human nature. Now, why should we despair of soon seeing tolerance (forgive this European word here) established in our country? Is it not practiced today in the Old World from Kamchatka to Iceland and from Lapland to the Apennines? Princes from the House of Hugues Capet[26] are the only great monarchs not to have welcomed it in their provinces yet. But in France, the unanimous voice of all enlightened men in the clergy, in the nobility, in the magistracy, and in commerce, is calling for this reform forcefully and tirelessly. Will these entreaties be fruitless? Should we not rather hope that the government will yield to reasons of justice and utility, and even that tolerance will be established in France more systematically and in greater conformity with natural justice, and that we will thereby erase the misfortune and perhaps the shame of having waited so long to follow the example of other peoples?

To be sure, the specific advantages of trade with America will diminish little by little. Europe will be left only with those resulting from an active and extensive trade between industrious and wealthy nations. But this change will be the work of several centuries, and by then the further progress of the human race will leave nothing to regret for enlightened nations of both the Old and New Worlds.

It is impossible that adding one more nation to the small number of those practicing an enlightened and active trade will not increase competition between them, the natural effect of which is to lower transportation costs; and this will benefit all nations, which have no other real interest than to obtain, in abundance and at the lowest possible price, goods that need or habit make necessary to them.

Finally, we should not believe that trade with America must be limited to what it is currently providing to Europe. How many materials does this immense land contain that are barely known today to our naturalists, even nearly unknown to its inhabitants, and the utility of which trade will soon make us discover? Even if the conjecture we venture here were not based on knowledge of several productions which, it is easy to predict, will one day become articles of trade, this hope should not be considered illusory. It would be entirely against the permanent order of nature for this vast continent to offer to Europe only useless or ordinary products.

Stern moralists will perhaps tell us that this benefit, which would just give us new needs, must be regarded as harmful;[27] but we will reply that, on the contrary, it will provide us with new resources to satisfy those needs to which nature has wished to subject us. Wherever and whenever great inequality in wealth exists, men will have artificial needs, and contagion from example will make them felt by the very people whom poverty prevents from satisfying them. Thus, to multiply the means of satisfying these artificial needs and make such means less costly is a good thing; it makes the effects of wealth inequality less perceptible and less dangerous to public tranquility; and if ever the slow but certain influence of a good system of laws can erase this inequality in Europe, artificial needs which inequality alone has created will disappear with it, or rather there will remain only what is needed to preserve the activity, the industriousness and curiosity necessary to the progress, and therefore the happiness, of the human race.

Certainly, we would have wished to be able to count an example of complete and unlimited freedom of trade set by a great nation among the benefits that will result from our relations with America. But although, regarding other political matters, these new republics have displayed more reason and intelligence than even the most enlightened nations, on the two important and closely related subjects of taxation and trade, they seem to have retained some remnants of the prejudices of the English nation. They do not appear to recognize clearly enough that it is in America's interest to grant all goods and nations complete freedom to come and go, to buy and sell without exception or privilege, regardless of whether European nations restore freedom of trade or keep commerce in chains or introduce new trade restrictions. Already misled by the example of mercantilist practices in Europe,[28] a few states have impeded trade with indirect taxes. They have not seen how easy it would be to institute and collect a direct tax on the product of the land in a country where landowners form a majority, where property is more equally distributed than in Europe, and where taxes are very low. Besides, what benefit would the equal citizens of a free state not find in a system under which no one, seeing what a new tax must cost him, would be fooled by arguments which, under vain pretexts, would tend to promote the institution of unnecessary ones?

Such a tax would not discourage new settlements since it is easy to set, as in France, a time limit before which newly cleared land would not be subject to it. The small amount of currency in circulation in America does not constitute a valid objection because, not only in America, where taxes are very low, but even in the most overtaxed nations, the amount of currency in metals or paper necessary to pay taxes represents a very small fraction of what is used in commercial transactions and in everyday life.

If one examines the history of the administration of the United States since the Declaration of Independence, one will not find equally well-conceived constitutions in all the states. There is none where some flaws cannot be observed, not all laws enacted since independence are equally just and wise. But no area of political or criminal law will present gross errors, oppressive or destructive principles. On the contrary, in financial and commercial operations, almost everything reveals a constant struggle between the old prejudices of Europe and the principles of justice and liberty so dear to this respectable nation: and often prejudices have prevailed.

However, while acknowledging these flaws, there is no doubt that the love Americans have for equality, their respect for liberty and property, and the form of their constitutions will forever prevent the establishment of prohibitions, either absolute or indirectly imposed through excessive duties, of exclusive trade privileges, of monopolies on certain commodities, of inspections that are so insulting and contrary to all the rights of citizens, of barbaric laws against fraud, of exclusive guilds of merchants or workers, in short, of everything the spirit of mercantilism and furor of universal regulation, to achieve universal oppression, have produced in Europe in the way of absurd vexations, and the American example will at least teach us to see their uselessness and injustice.

I have not mentioned the tobacco trade between France and America because it is not carried on by France but by the company holding a monopoly over it, whose interests are entirely foreign to those of the nation, when they are not frankly contrary to them. With whichever trading partner and in whatever form, such trade is always equally harmful. A company will buy only from another, and even if a fraction of the benefit resulting from exchanging goods for goods as opposed to goods for currency were still to be found in purchasing this commodity from America, incidental costs of all kinds inseparable from a monopoly are so much greater than this benefit that it would become almost negligible.

Conclusion

Such have been my reflections on the influence of the American Revolution. I do not think I have exaggerated its importance or allowed myself to be carried away by the enthusiasm inspired by the noble and moving example this new people is setting for the world.

Supplement to Filippo Mazzei's *Researches on the United States* (1788)

Recent news from the United States requires a supplement.[1] It is hoped that this addition will not displease those eager to be informed of the affairs of this country, so that they can form likely conjectures about the future.

We will first comment upon the uprising which took place in the state of Massachusetts.[2]

Europe gets its news about the United States from English gazettes. Well-informed Americans have constantly remarked that by taking the opposite view to what these gazettes claim concerning their affairs, one would get details as accurate as those that could be obtained from whomever would take the most scrupulous care to be truthful. Even with the intention of always disfiguring the truth, it is impossible not to stumble upon it sometimes. This is what English gazetteers have experienced lately. After informing Europe, for several consecutive years, about imaginary uprisings that allegedly took place in this part of America, they have at last announced a real one, only the details are inaccurate. We said in the fourth chapter of the last part[3] that there was discontent in the state of Massachusetts and gave some indication of several reasons for it, such as the impossibility, for many people, of paying taxes and their private debts without ruining themselves. The prodigious amount of foreign goods which flooded this country as soon as peace was signed, and innumerable payments made to English creditors for debts incurred before the war, drained it of currency. The inability to pay taxes, having lasted several years, had caused a buildup of arrears, more or less according to the circumstances, and public needs forced the government to demand payment with rigor. In some counties where the pressures of government and creditors were causing more commotion, a few ill-intentioned people, or rather a few people prompted by despair, sought to take advantage of a situation of social unrest. Their leader was a former sergeant major in our army,[4] named Shays.

Their first step was to summon the citizens, the wisest and most sensible of whom stayed home. In these assemblies it was agreed to close the courts, suspend the collection of taxes, put paper currency into circulation, and change part of the government. All these proposals seemed popular. The courts' inaction left debtors in peace. The issuing of paper currency offered the prospect of conveniently paying back debts, and the changes intended in government were designed to reduce its expenses, which by the way are very low.

As these men had no hope of winning the support of a majority of citizens, and thereby of being able to act legally, they used violence. They marched in great numbers, weapons in hand, and in some counties put a stop to the course of justice, without causing any other disorder. The governor immediately called together the general court.[i] It was resolved to levy a corps of fifteen hundred men, under the command of General Lincoln, and to reinforce it with as many militiamen as necessary to disperse the riot and restore order.

In the meantime, General Shepard had assembled approximately eight hundred militiamen in order to protect the arsenal in Springfield. Shays, accompanied by twelve hundred men, having called on him to surrender, he responded with a volley of artillery which killed four men, wounded several and dispersed all the rest. They reassembled later some distance away; but General Lincoln, by an extremely quick march, ended the fight in an instant.[ii] A high hill prevented him from taking them by surprise; nevertheless, he took a hundred and fifty prisoners and dispersed the others completely, without shedding a drop of blood. Shays escaped with seventeen of the most seditious men, and it is believed they are now in Canada. The others went back home.

The first setback they met with was dealt them by a company of volunteers which had left Boston riding at full speed. It captured three of the leaders and took them to jail.

As for the fugitives, the government of Massachusetts offered a reward to whoever would arrest them, and the governments of New Hampshire and Vermont,[iii] where they were believed to have taken refuge, did the same thing.

---

i. The reader will remember that the legislative assembly in that state is called *general court*.

ii. The night before this engagement, he traveled thirty miles from eight in the evening to nine in the morning, although the roads were covered with a thick blanket of snow.

iii. The conduct of the state of Vermont on this occasion must be compared with what the gazetteers have claimed on the matter.

The turmoil once appeased, the general court set up a *Commission* to look into the matter and to judge who would be worthy of a pardon, according to justice.

These men had not ventured the slightest act of violence against a single individual. Since the majority had acted in blindness and had no evil intentions, the small number of those of ill will could not have behaved differently without unmasking themselves and ruining their plan.

According to the latest news, the commissioners had already pardoned seven hundred and ninety men, and only a small number of leaders, who had been put in jail in their respective counties to be questioned and judged, were considered guilty. It is even believed that the general court will grant a pardon to several among those who will be sentenced to death, and that only three or four of the guiltiest will be executed. It could be feared that a general pardon might lead to regard the fact as of little importance, or to suppose weakness in the government.

In Europe, the uprising in Massachusetts has provided material for declamations against popular governments. We use the word "declamations" and not "arguments" since reflection would have made those who composed them see that this uprising proves the excellence of popular governments, from whatever perspective they are considered.

During the eleven years that the thirteen American governments have been in existence, only one has seen a rebellion arise, and it is the one I have just mentioned. Let us suppose that the same thing happens successively in the other states after a similar length of time, it would take a period of one hundred and forty-three years for one uprising to take place in each and every state. In what other governments have uprisings been as rare? If one casts a glance at the history of Asian governments, one will see that the most frightful despotism could not prevent them. Let anyone choose from among despotic, monarchical and mixed governments, three of the best known, for example, Constantinople, France and England; and examine the uprisings that took place under each of them, I am not saying in the space of one hundred and forty-three years, but only during the last eleven years; and then compare them with all the events of this kind that have occurred in the United States; it will be agreed that, in comparison with other nations, a profound tranquility has reigned among us during this period. I have said enough on the number of uprisings; let us now consider their causes, course and effects.

The rebellion in Massachusetts owes its origin to a series of unfortunate circumstances which had built up over time and came to an unbearable crisis because of considerable levies of money occasioned by a sudden change of situation. Once this crisis comes to an end, the natural course of human affairs gives hope that the same catastrophe will not happen again.

The harm caused by the uprising consisted of the temporary suspension of a few courts, and an engagement during which, as already said, four of the rebels were killed and several wounded; and it will end with the execution of three or four more who, in all likelihood, will be fated to serve as examples. What is all this compared with what takes place during uprisings in England? What a difference with the effects of Lord Gordon's riots[5] alone! That event was not brought about by any misfortune, and the purpose in view was only to force parliament to revoke an act of justice. The consequences of the uprising that took place in Glasgow approximately two months ago[6] and is hardly talked about, were much more serious than those of the rebellion in Massachusetts, which has gotten so much attention in Europe, as if everything there were in flames, since in Glasgow, besides five dead and several wounded counted among the rioters, the first magistrate of the town and others who had come running to appease the turmoil were also among the injured, and finally, the property of many private citizens was affected.

Those who rioted in Massachusetts did not use violence against any individual, his person or his property, and paid everywhere the fair price for what they needed. But what should be more striking than anything else to those who would want the administration to exert the full weight of its authority, is the way the inhabitants acted to appease the turmoil. In what other governments would citizens, to achieve this end, display such great and universal zeal? Where would companies of volunteers be seen arming themselves and riding at full speed to defend the government? In short, this uprising, about which so-called politicians have talked in such ridiculous fashion, is perhaps one of the most convincing proofs that to maintain order in a nation, the care thereof must be left to the nation itself.

It is time now to convince ourselves that a nation where equality of rights reigns will support its government if it believes it is good, change it when it believes it is bad, and amend it when it finds it deficient; that for this the majority does not need to use violence, and that violence used by a minority will naturally be impotent; that what is called the populace in Europe is a class of men which does not and cannot exist under our governments; that national dissensions cannot grow deep roots in a country where odious and unjust social distinctions are unknown; that a class of men excluded from the rights of citizenship must be at least indifferent to the established form of government, when it is not an enemy to it; that finally, the only way to make the preservation of order dear to the people is to make order alone essential to their happiness and safety.

In the second part of this work we mentioned the considerable progress that has been observed in all the states in favor of freedom of conscience, as well as what remained to be done to make this freedom complete. Since that time, the general assembly of Virginia having undertaken to examine the new code that was also mentioned, passed the law proposed in it, so that freedom of conscience now rests on the best possible foundation. This was the effect of a remonstrance by the people, which we inserted into the notes to the second part, letter G: another example providing evidence against those who so fear the influence of the people in matters of government.

The comte de Mirabeau rightly said, before Europe was informed of the passage of this law, "You speak of tolerance! And there is no country on earth, without excepting the new American republics, where it is enough to practice social virtues for a man to enjoy all the benefits of society."[iv]

Now at least Virginia must be excepted, since in this state religion is distinct from the responsibilities and rights of citizenship. It is to be desired that soon all the American republics can be included in the same exception.

The law relative to inheritance has also just been approved in Virginia. There is no longer any partiality in favor of primogeniture or male heirs. Other useful regulations are known to have been adopted of which the particular details have not yet reached us. The same reforms are being enacted in all the other states, more or less, according to the circumstances; and if Europe were accurately informed of what is happening there, it would see gradual improvements everywhere, and would be persuaded that the dire prophecies of so-called legislators have no other basis than a craze for ranting, whatever the pretext.

Lately, the consoling news was received that the general assembly of South Carolina had prohibited the importation of slaves for three years. It appears that the friends of universal freedom did not believe they should insist on a permanent prohibition, for fear of shocking the contrary opinion too violently; but we hope that this prohibition will be put in place before the expiration of the present law, and it will probably not be long before

---

iv. Letter from the comte de Mirabeau to ★★★ concerning Messrs. de Cagliostro & Lavater. Berlin, 1786.

North Carolina and Georgia, the only states where the importation of slaves is still permitted, also do the same.

The peace treaty between the United States and Great Britain[7] has not yet been fully implemented on either side. Europe has not been better informed on this point than on the others. A faithful statement of the facts will be the simplest and surest way to refute the falsehoods that have been spread.

When peace was concluded, there were in New York approximately four thousand slaves, most of them belonging to the inhabitants of Virginia. Before the evacuation of the town by the English troops, the slaves were to be returned in compliance with the peace treaty. The request having been made to Sir Carleton, commander in chief, he replied that he was aware of the conditions in the treaty but had promised them freedom and did not want to break his word. He took them with him and left it to the government of Great Britain to reimburse their value. It is a painful thought that Great Britain's first wrong regarding noncompliance with the treaty originated in an act which does honor to its commander.

During the war, the functions of the courts were suspended in several American states, and by law, all of them strictly forbade English creditors to take any legal action against their debtors. An article of the treaty states that all legal prohibitions concerning English creditors will be lifted. Upon General Carleton's refusal, the general assembly of Virginia let them continue. Congress complained and the assembly then made the law mentioned in chapter 5, by which English creditors could recover their due in seven equal yearly payments, including interest since the peace.

This law attended to the mutual interest of debtors and creditors, since among debtors many are in the situation of ruining themselves without being able to satisfy their creditors if they are not granted different terms. The body of creditors acknowledged this in London with our ministers to the courts of France and England; but the English secretary of state, who at first had seemed to go along with the negotiation, evaded any further discussion on the subject.

It is fitting to note that in western parts of the territory which, according to the peace treaty, belongs to the United States, the English had a few forts which they are still keeping, although according to the treaty they should have evacuated them. These forts are useful to them to trade with the savages; they can also, by this means, more easily incline them to back up their designs. It is not unlikely that this government is well pleased to have a pretext to hold on to these forts, and perhaps with other plans in view, which cannot long remain hidden.

Virginia did not have the right to maintain the law which closed the courts to English creditors, nor to substitute the other law, which allows them to recover their due in seven installments. The fairness of this course of action does not justify it. The peace treaty states that the courts will be open and admits of no condition. In truth, the first wrong lies with the English regarding the slaves they have neither returned nor paid for; but Virginia, instead of following this example, should have appealed to Congress, to which alone belongs the right to handle and decide matters related to the confederation. If any one state had the right to interfere, there would soon be anarchy.

The result of the discussions between Congress and the English government can be found in a letter from Lord Carmarthen, secretary of state of the king of England, to Mr. Adams, minister plenipotentiary of the United States to that court. Lord Carmarthen implies in this letter that Great Britain will not fulfill the conditions of the treaty as long as we will not have fulfilled them ourselves, and he mentions circumstances in which, according to him, various states have deviated from them. On September 22, 1786, a vindication against the assertions contained in this letter was published in Philadelphia regarding the state of Pennsylvania. It says that, since peace was signed, English creditors have never found the courts closed to sue their debtors, and that exceptions have always related only to domestic debts. The following observation can be read in this text: "British merchants since the peace have had full scope in Pennsylvania, against the lands as well as goods of their debtors, which is not so in England, in like cases, lands there not being liable to sale for debts."[8] The vindication refers to court registers as evidence of cases that have been tried since the peace, and that are brought against English creditors every day.

There is more: as an additional precaution the law specifies an explicit exception "for debts owed to the subjects of Great Britain by the citizens of this state."

The priority for Congress has been to attend to what was most important to us, that is, the implementation of our side of the peace treaty, in order to put a stop to any kind of pretext. It is hoped that the reader will not be displeased to find here in its entirety the letter sent on this topic by Congress to the first magistrate of each of the thirteen states.

[We omit this letter of April 13, 1787, by Arthur St. Clair, president of Congress.][9]

Several states have already passed the law Congress recommends in its letter, and in all probability the others will follow suit as soon as their legislative bodies are assembled. After that, it will be impossible for the designs of Great Britain to remain hidden for long. I wish to risk a prediction on this subject, based on the knowledge I believe I have of my fellow citizens. I dare to predict, therefore, that an insulting pride which can sometimes triumph over the patience of others, or over their excessive prudence, will be absolutely without effect in America, despite the current state of its finances.

We said, in chapter 5 of this last part, that the various states were going to send deputies to a *Convention* in order to discuss the means to give the confederation the most solidity, stability, activity and energy possible. The *Convention* was held in Philadelphia; it lasted for four months and ended in proposing to the states the draft of a new federal constitution which is included below together with the letter from the president addressing it to the president of Congress.

Among the various reasons which prevented this assembly from convening earlier, the main one must be attributed to article 13 of the Articles of Confederation, which states that no "alteration at any time hereafter [shall] be made in any of them [the articles of this confederation]; unless such alteration be agreed to in a Congress of the United States, and be afterwards confirmed by the legislatures of every State." Several states therefore asserted that since Congress had the right to deliberate on necessary reforms, there was no need to convene a special *Convention* on the matter. Finally, they agreed with the others on a *Convention*, for two reasons that can only be approved of. To be a member of a *Convention*, any citizen can be elected, even if he holds an office in the republic; thus Virginia sent to the *Convention* in question Mr. Edmund Randolph, currently governor, Dr. McClurg, member of the executive council, Mr. James Madison, member of Congress, Mr. George Wythe and Mr. John Blair, judges on the court of chancery. Several who had completely retired from public life did not refuse to serve on an extraordinary occasion: thus General Washington and Mr. George Mason were both delegated by the same state.

[We omit the letter dated September 17, 1787, by Washington, president of the Constitutional Convention, addressing to the president of Congress the project of a federal constitution,[10] as well as the text of the constitution itself.]

The *Convention* did not expect, and the letter from the president indicates it clearly, that the federal constitution would win the full and complete approval of each state. On the contrary, I think that each will make useful objections. The topic of this work requires that I make my opinion known, and I will try to present it as briefly as possible.

The first federal constitution, entitled the Articles of Confederation,[11] is such that any society of sensible and virtuous men could consider itself honored to have conceived it. What few flaws it contains are the result of a laudable precaution, and besides they are easy to correct. It seems to me that it could have been preserved as a monument worthy of respect, as the fundamental basis of our union, adding to it what it lacks to bring it to the degree of perfection which is possible to achieve. The proposed constitution disregards it entirely, so that whoever is not familiar with it might form of it an idea altogether contrary to the truth.

In the first constitution, the power of Congress is neither broad enough in some cases, nor specific enough in others. The constitution that is proposed makes it exceed, in various circumstances, the limits of a purely federative government. The first concentrates legislative and executive matters in a single body; the new one goes so far as to divide into several branches the legislative body alone. To correct and perfect the first constitution as much as possible, it would be enough to change article 8, as proposed by Congress on April 18, 1783, to separate legislative and executive powers, and to grant Congress the right to levy sums of money, regulate trade, prevent any state of the union from minting money, or giving legal value to paper, or any other kind of fictitious currency, and ordain what will be the required majority of the states, so that absent ones cannot influence deliberations.

Corrections and additions necessary to make this first constitution as perfect as possible are included in the second, but alongside several others to which I hope my fellow citizens will pay the attention they deserve.

Article 1, § 1. *All legislative Powers herein granted shall be vested in a Congress of the United States, which shall consist of a Senate and House of Representatives.* Even if one agreed that it is useful to divide the legislative power in the constitution of a single state, it would not follow that the same thing should be done in a federal constitution. The letter I have just mentioned tries to justify this complication on the grounds that it is not appropriate to grant so much power to a single body. It would be as difficult to prove that complicating the system would provide enough of a check, as it is easy to show that the necessary legislative power can reside in a single chamber without any danger. This fear, which can appear founded when dealing with a genuine legislative body, cannot seriously be alleged here:

1. Because the power of a federal congress is by nature much more limited than that of a legislative body, which lessens the danger.

2. Because the coming together of all the parts of this congress is easier, because it forms a body that is much more separated from the citizens, which makes the remedy less efficient.

The reader will easily discover, here as elsewhere, various other reasons, unstated or simply hinted at, the discussion of which would make this supplement too long.

§ 2. *The House of Representatives shall be composed of Members chosen every second Year by the People of the several States.* In most states, the people, convinced that the majority of the inhabitants of a state cannot know well enough who the citizens most worthy of holding certain offices in the republic are, has prudently left their selection to its representatives. No doubt the same people will not imagine it can do better when choosing men who must administer the affairs of the union and deal with foreign powers. Moreover, it is hard to understand why Congress should prescribe the mode of election. Each state must hand over to the confederation such power as could be harmful to the others, if it acted on its own; but it is impossible that the mode of election in one state be a matter of concern to any other. Finally, uniformity on this point would be absurd, since experience shows that in some states of moderate size the population is fit to participate in some elections which, in others, it believes itself obliged to entrust to representatives. The law of the confederation could just preclude certain conditions, such as the election of a family in perpetuity, of a deputy for life, and so forth, since a state can require another, without detriment to its independence, to proscribe everything which could be contrary to the general freedom.

§ 3. *The Senate of the United States shall be composed of two Senators from each State, chosen by the Legislature thereof for six Years; and each Senator shall have one Vote.* Here, several observations arise:

1. The term of six years is too long, since it is an invariable fact that three years of absence are enough to alienate in large part the trust of the people, a very considerable flaw in our governments.

2. There is not a single plausible reason to support the difference between the election of senators and that of representatives.[12] Every complication in the system, every distinction is harmful by nature, and can only be justified by necessity. The other distinction between the Senate and the House of

Representatives, pertaining to the influence of the various states, is a source of discord. We have already seen that the number of representatives is to be proportional to the number of inhabitants, and that each representative, like each senator, is to have one vote. Let us examine the grounds upon which equality in one case, and difference in the other, are founded.

Several people are of the opinion that the influence of a state in the affairs of the union must be proportional to the taxes paid in that state; others think that perfect equality, without regard for size or population, must be preferred. Until now, all the states have each had one vote, and the constitution that has just been proposed follows the same principle with respect to the Senate, adopting the other for the House of Representatives. The influence of Virginia, compared with that of Rhode Island and Delaware, will thus be in a ratio of ten to one in the House of Representatives and perfectly equal in the Senate; and since resolutions of one of these bodies must be submitted for approval to the other, it is unlikely that such an expedient will produce the desired effect; if the smaller states believe themselves harmed by a resolution of the representatives, they will reject it in the Senate.

It is a mistake to delude oneself into thinking that contrary principles can be reconciled. Such expedients will sometimes be useful, perhaps, as temporary remedies; they will never form the basis of a very solid structure. It is therefore necessary to decide in favor of one side or the other. Principles must be firm and certain, and everything must tend to uphold them. It would be desirable that the states be equal, or their inequality small; but since it is not so, one must at least endeavor to reduce the harm instead of adding to it. To be sure, the problem is difficult to solve. The strength of the arguments set forth on both sides in Congress in 1777 left wise and unprejudiced minds undecided. The need for unanimity led these great men to join together in favor of the equality of individual votes, and the *Convention* has just adopted this expedient of which I fear the consequences. Whoever would find the true solution and present it clearly and decisively would do a great service for America, and perhaps even for Europe, where the considerable progress of philosophy gives rise to the hope of seeing one day a confederation become established, which could infinitely lessen the suffering of humankind.

§ 6. *The Senators and Representatives shall receive a Compensation for their Services, to be ascertained by Law, and paid out of the Treasury of the United States.* The laws of the union are made by Congress. I hope it will never be allowed to set its own salary. From this could result a dangerous abuse for the future, and too much zeal would perhaps produce, as to the present, the opposite effect, that is to say, too much disinterestedness, two extremes that are to be avoided equally. There can also be some harm in leaving each state responsible for this payment; but if uniformity is desired, the salary must be set by a *Convention*, and not by Congress itself.

§ 9. *The Privilege of the Writ of Habeas Corpus shall not be suspended, unless when in Cases of Rebellion or Invasion the public Safety may require it.* The declaration of rights, in all the states, proclaims that this privilege must never be suspended. If it was deemed appropriate to mention it in the federal constitution, it should only have been in order to further demonstrate how much in the interest of the safety of citizens it is that it should always be considered sacred. During the Revolution, there was a period (it was toward the end of 1776) when the instability of governments and several other circumstances called for its suspension; but it was not granted, despite the singularly critical state in which we found ourselves, and for reasons which can no longer exist. It is never very inconvenient, nor very dangerous, to be required to bring to trial according to the law a citizen who has been arrested, to have him appear before judges, and to give him the means to defend himself as soon as he is arrested.

No Tax or Duty shall be laid on Articles exported from any State. It is legitimate that Congress not have such a power, but it must not have the right to forbid a state to use this power if the latter deems it advisable, because the damage caused by such regulation would only affect the state where it would exist. For the same reason it would be out of place for the union to share in the proceeds of such a tax, as proposed in section 10.

No Money shall be drawn from the Treasury, but in Consequence of Appropriations made by Law; and a regular Statement and Account of the Receipts and Expenditures of all public Money shall be published from time to time. An unspecified period of time to account for the use of public funds can lead to the most pernicious effects. It is necessary to inform the people of the state of public finances at fixed and short intervals. Every year would not be too short an interval; it would not be so long either as to make it impossible for the nation to verify the facts and make sure of the good conduct of its administrators. If Congress is granted the freedom to render its account whenever it pleases, as the vague expression "from time to time" indicates, and to establish and collect taxes every time it sees fit, it might as well be granted unlimited power, since nothing will be able to oppose those who can dispose of the wealth of the states.

As for article 2, which is entirely devoted to the election, functions, remuneration, and so forth, of the president, one must observe:

1. The mode of election of this president, which tends to favor the individual most in the public eye over the most meritorious; and one knows that true merit is in general less recognized than false brilliance and quackery.

2. The power he is granted to command in person the army and navy, whereas he should only be entrusted with the choice of commanders and be barred from commanding in person.

3. The executive power given to him alone without the assistance of any council, something unheard of, dangerous to the public good, and to which a wise and judicious president will never aspire, since being answerable for his actions, he would run many risks if, for difficult and delicate affairs, he was deprived of the resource of a council whose opinion, having become his guarantee, could be used to justify his conduct.

4. The possibility of reelecting him with no limit,[13] which would set a very bad example, even in the case of the greatest man nature could produce. It would be better to renounce the benefit of having such a prodigy as leader of the confederation than to accustom the people to always seeing the same individual in this office. One step further and soon we would have a king of Poland,[14] with the terrible danger of seeing him change one day into a hereditary Stadtholder.[15]

Article 3, § 2. The method proposed to settle disputes between two or several states can give rise to systematic intrigues, with very pernicious effects, whereas the one already present in the Articles of Confederation is the best possible[16] (see the notes to the second part). As for the right to judge cases involving citizens of different states or a citizen of the union and a foreign citizen, it must be left to the courts of the state where the facts are easiest to verify, and not given to the federal courts, as proposed in this section. It also seems, according to the same section, that civil cases may be prosecuted without a trial by jury, a serious oversight it is essential to correct.[17]

There is no apparent reason for the arithmetic proportion according to which the minimum age for holding various offices is set.[v] This precaution, misplaced and insulting to the young, is diametrically opposed to our experience. How many young people could we not count whose exemplary

---

v. The proposed federal constitution requires twenty-five years of age in order to be a representative, thirty to be a senator, and thirty-five to be president.

conduct belies such suspicion? I will only cite, among the ancients, Scipio Africanus who, as early as twenty-two years of age, stunned the world with his virtue, wisdom and moderation, as well as his courage and skill at military leadership.

Lately in the House of Commons of Great Britain, a young man of twenty-two was seen proving himself suddenly superior to a father whose reputation has been too brilliant for his talents to need to be mentioned, and he is now seen managing the affairs of that kingdom with applause to which envy itself has been forced to yield.[18]

The conduct of a young hero, who, at barely nineteen, crossed the ocean to come to our aid at the most critical time during the Revolution, is more than enough to make us ashamed of our reluctance to admit young people to the offices of the republic.[19]

Among the young Americans I know, I could name a large number who confirm my opinion, if various considerations did not prevent me from doing so.

If biased laws do not give rise to prejudices, they at least strengthen them and allow them to grow. In every country where public opinion belittles or discourages the young, it should come as no surprise that they lack a sense of emulation, a flaw that is ordinarily attributed to youth with the same injustice which causes the consequences of a bad education to be regarded as natural flaws in women.[20]

Bias in favor of advanced age all too often leads to a preference for mediocre men, even many who owe the respect and regard in which they are held to a certain tone of solemnity along with a severe countenance, over young people of great merit. No one in general feels inclined to prefer a young man, unless his merit is exceptional. Why then make on this matter an unjust law which can be harmful to the public good, and must be acknowledged as unnecessary even by its most zealous advocates? The fear that people of mature age have of the young must come either from vanity, which often operates unconsciously, or from a false notion which makes them mistake for the effect of consummate wisdom the cooling of this courage and nobility of the soul which do honor to the human race, which, always useful to the republic, are sometimes its only support, and which are usually the prerogative of young people. If one insisted on prescribing age-restrictive laws regarding public offices, it would be less harmful to exclude those in whom the inevitable weakness of the body almost always has an effect upon the soul.

With respect to the years of residence required to be eligible for certain offices, I do not think it is necessary to repeat what I have said elsewhere to show that such precautions owe their origin in large part to prejudices learned from early childhood, that they are useless, unjust, and reveal a shameful narrow-mindedness.

The privilege of pardoning criminals convicted for certain offences, granted to the president in the second section of article 2, cannot fail to open the door to intrigue and abuse of influence. Just as Congress should never be judge in a trial, the right to grant pardon should not be given to the president; at most, it could be given to Congress itself, and only in the case of treason against the confederation, or for military offences. Besides, it would be best not to grant this right at all. Beccaria[21] proves clearly that this kind of mistaken humaneness is nothing other than asylum for impunity and therefore a source of crimes.

Article 7. *The Ratification of the Conventions of nine States, shall be sufficient for the Establishment of this Constitution between the States so ratifying the Same.* It would be better if three-quarters of the states were required, as in article 5 for future changes; otherwise there would be much to fear if four of the most populous states were to contemplate secession. The population of four states such as Virginia, Massachusetts, Pennsylvania, and New York or Maryland, compared with that of the other nine, is in a ratio of thirty-two to thirty-three. Excluding Massachusetts and including the other four the ratio is thirty to thirty-five, but by their geographic position they encircle New Jersey and Delaware and divide the seven remaining states, of which four are to the north and three to the south.

I did not intend to examine scrupulously everything which would perhaps deserve a discussion; for example, whether the power granted to Congress is not such as to make the governments of the individual states almost powerless; but however important the preceding observations may seem to me, I am far from thinking that the proposed federal constitution earned the assent of so many men endowed with zeal, knowledge and wisdom without powerful reasons. It seems unlikely that during four months of debate on a single subject, they have not turned their attention to everything related to it and examined it thoroughly. He who has not participated in this assembly is hardly in a position to judge the motives that may have led each of these men to give this document his full and complete approval, even though perhaps none of them believed it free of imperfections.

From a distance it is hard to see the particular causes which stand in the way of general principles. The reader familiar with the true principles of legislation and government will blame me for having raised no objection to the power granted Congress to regulate trade and levy sums of money in the respective states. No doubt commerce must be absolutely free and exempt from all taxes. It is also certain that Congress ought to set the amount of taxation and make the request, with no other right than to force payment, according to fixed procedures set in advance by law. But the circumstances in which we find ourselves require that it have the right, for some time, to levy a direct tax and lay some taxes on foreign goods. This time period should certainly be limited; because reasons which make it necessary to deviate from general principles must at some point come to an end when they do not originate in absolute need, produced by the geography of the country: for example, a direct tax on landed property could not be the only government income in the state of Genoa where nature, instead of land, offers only rocks, so to speak, nor in the state of Holland, where it offers expanses of water on all sides.

In our country, as long as the low price of land prevents the growth of manufacturing, or at least as long as foreign debts, private and public, are not paid off, it will be appropriate to add a moderate tax on foreign goods to direct taxation, not only to increase public income, but also to force the consumer to use these goods as little as possible, since without much thrift in this respect the proceeds of our exports cannot be sufficient to offset the cost of our imports and pay off already-existing debt; hence the fact that we must export our hard currency, which necessarily entails a loss in the exchange and an inability to pay taxes.

Our situation therefore requires that we make a few exceptions to general principles. But it would be advisable that the preamble of each law instituting an exception state the reasons for it, in order to convince the people that it is an evil made necessary by the circumstances and to make them see its end, which they would naturally be eager to hasten.

The letter from the president of the *Convention* to the president of Congress clearly implies that these wise and judicious men, in proposing to the states this system of legislation, thought they were offering them not the most perfect system but the best possible under current circumstances. The reader will see a more positive proof of this in the reflections Dr. Franklin addressed to his colleagues on the last day of the session.[22] When nothing remained to be done but sign the constitution project, such was approximately the speech he addressed to them. Whoever knows his style will not find it difficult to believe that this speech was either copied immediately in abbreviated form as he was delivering it, or memorized, perhaps word for word, by the person who communicated it.

"Mr. President,

We have spent a long time together. We have discussed every objection that could be foreseen. With so many different and opposed interests, it was impossible for everyone to obtain everything he desired. We assembled intending to make mutual sacrifices for the public good, and we have finally succeeded in acting in concert and laying some foundations. We would gain nothing by delaying, and it is important to adopt a plan. I confess that there are several parts of this Constitution which I do not at present approve, but I am not sure I shall never approve them: For having lived long, I have experienced many instances of being obliged by better information or fuller consideration, to change opinions even on important subjects, which I once thought right, but found to be otherwise. In the present circumstances, I have, after careful consideration, changed my mind on several points in favor of which I thought myself at first resolutely decided. This makes me less obstinate on the rest. I may have been wrong. The general principle which presided over our deliberations is now my rule. Thus I consent, Sir, to this Constitution because I expect no better, and because I am not sure that it is not the best. The opinions I have had of its errors, I sacrifice to the public good—I have never whispered a syllable of them abroad. Within these walls they were born, and here they shall die. I hope therefore that for our own sakes as a part of the people, and for the sake of posterity, we shall act heartily and unanimously in recommending this Constitution wherever our influence may extend, and turn our future thoughts and endeavors to the means of having it well administered. On the whole, Sir, I cannot help expressing a wish that every member of the Convention who may still have objections to it, would with me, on this occasion, doubt a little of his own infallibility—and to make manifest our unanimity, put his name to this instrument.[vi] Refusing would remind me of a certain French lady, who in a

---

vi. Three delegates, two from Virginia and one from New York, who did not see fit to sign, left the assembly in order not to prevent unanimity [but several delegates had already left the convention without signing; in fact, out of a total of fifty-five, sixteen delegates from eight states did not sign the Constitution]. As for the state of Rhode Island, it took no part in it, and I will say nothing of the motives ascribed to its conduct. Casting a glance at the map of the United States, one becomes convinced that this state could not be of great weight on the other side of the scale, and the rule of probability suggests that the more reasonable part of its population will soon prevail, since extraordinary insight is not necessary to realize that its existence depends on its union with the allied republics, and that without this union the protection of a foreign power could not prevent its ruin. The state of Rhode Island has approximately sixty thousand inhabitants.

dispute with her sister, said, 'I don't know how it happens, Sister, but I meet with nobody but myself, that's always in the right'—*Il n'y a que moi qui a [sic] toujours raison.*"vii,23

The fear of granting too much power to Congress produced the flaw in the first federal constitution, and the harm resulting from it probably caused the drafters of the second to go too far concerning this topic. No doubt they hoped that, when it would come to adopting it, the legislative assemblies of the individual states would step back a little and cut this power down to the true level prudence requires. They themselves will perhaps be the first to propose appropriate changes.

The most dangerous item is the power granted the president to command the armies in person, and even more so the possibility of reelecting him with no limit. If this part of the constitution is not amended soon, our descendants could have a serious reason to complain about us. The office of president would become so prominent that we would have to fear, among many other dangers, that some European courts would see fit to meddle with the elections, as for a long time has been the case in Poland, to the great detriment, and I might even say to the irreparable detriment, of such a vast and fertile country. Since an item of such importance must not, it seems, have resulted from carelessness, it will be profitable to ponder the motives which may have guided these great men in this respect, and examine whether the same motives can make it desirable to postpone changes on this matter.

Lack of vigor has produced a very detrimental inaction. To remedy this as must be, more than ordinary vigor is needed. This idea is consistent with general experience. Our lucky star has protected a man whose prudence and virtue deserve all our trust. General Washington is healthy and strong and not more than fifty-five years old. It will be difficult to find a single voice against him in the United States.viii He has expressed, it is true, his resolve to spend the rest of his days in private life; but the voice of his native land will tell him that, had he sworn as much before the altars, such an oath would be null every time the welfare of his country would require his services. All who know him well, far from expecting from him a stubborn refusal, will

vii. The duchesse de la Ferté said one day to Mademoiselle de Launay, later Madame de Staal, "In truth, my dear girl, I meet with nobody but myself, that's always in the right" (*Memoirs of Madame de Staal*).

viii. Characters of this stamp, although very rare, are not extremely so however; but no one is as universally known as General Washington.

anticipate with pleasure the time when this virtuous citizen wishes for a *Convention* to be elected to give the final touch to the federal constitution and reduce to within just limits the election and responsibilities of his eminent office, which he will be allowed to leave, because renewing him would set a most dangerous example. It is not necessary to have a prophetic mind to forecast this event, moderate insight is enough along with knowledge of our current situation and of the character of our fellow citizens.

Among the various affairs of the union presently requiring a prompt and efficient energy, one must not lose sight of the apparent dispositions of Great Britain. All the details coming out of that country regarding ours tend only to harm us throughout Europe. Our minister to that court is treated with affected neglect by the government, and for its part that government has not yet sent any representative to the United States. Men in high office there are heard discussing our alleged desire to return to the old dominion, and they say that if we asked we would be refused, whereas the schemes and insinuations of many British subjects throughout the United States betray diametrically opposite views. In Massachusetts, it is commonly thought that these schemes helped in no small way to bring about the uprising we mentioned.

Their actions relative to the Indians and the Barbary pirates seem to augur nothing good. It is enough for us to see them keep outposts which they have been under obligation to evacuate for four years, to be unable to put much of our trust in their dispositions. But it would not be surprising if a change in the direction of affairs pertaining to the confederation were followed by a change in their conduct toward us, considering the deep veneration that has reigned for some time in that country for everything *expedient*.

Europe has seen all the efforts made to predispose it against us on the subject of the latest *Convention*. One of the tales told of two alleged factions in the election of the president, of their extreme zeal, and maintained that General Washington had won by a single vote over Dr. Franklin. Nothing is further from the truth than these details. There was not a shadow of rivalry; on the contrary, Dr. Franklin was the first to propose General Washington; he accompanied him himself, with many others, to his seat, after our hero's extreme modesty could no longer resist the warm entreaties of his colleagues.

The content of this work compels me to inform the reader of the latest related news from America.

Last May, the domestic debt of the confederation had been cut down by eleven million dollars, thanks to various taxes imposed by the respective states which could be paid in federal paper currency. At that time, land sales began; five million dollars' worth has already been sold, so that the domestic debt is now reduced to twelve. Since paper currency is accepted as payment and written off as a loss in private contracts,[24] there is reason to hope that in this way the domestic debt will soon be paid off. Then it will be possible to sell land at lower prices and for hard currency, and to use such sales to pay off foreign debts.

We have just learned that no one has been executed in connection with the uprising in Massachusetts; two or three among the guiltiest men were led to the gallows where, contrary to all expectations, they were read their pardon. The conduct of the government caused general satisfaction and order is perfectly restored.

According to the latest news, the general assembly of New York was about to consent to the independence of Vermont, and it was believed North Carolina would not be long in doing the same for Frankland.[25] As for Kentucky, it is said that its inhabitants, whose number is currently estimated close to sixty thousand, think it is still too early to contemplate emancipation. In this case, they will remain under tutelage for a few more years, and without a doubt gazetteers will not fail to take advantage of this circumstance to spread rumors of anarchy and confusion.

Ideas on Despotism:
For the Benefit of Those Who Pronounce This Word
Without Understanding It (1789)

1

Despotism comes from the Greek word δεσπότης, which means master. There is *despotism* whenever men have masters, that is to say, are subjected to the arbitrary will of other men.

2

Despotism by one man alone is a fiction of the mind; but despotism by a small number over a large number is very common and has two causes: the ease with which a small number can join together, and its wealth, with which it can buy other forces.

If one examines the history of countries where it has been thought that despotism by one man existed, one will always see a class or several bodies of men who share with him his power. In Turkey, the Janissaries and the cast of legal professionals; in Rome, the Praetorian Guard and the twelve armies stationed along the borders; in France, the twelve parliaments; in Prussia, the army; in Russia, the regiments of the guards and the great lords.[i]

---

i. This is not to say that a conqueror, a great general, or this or that king cannot really be the sole master, as often in a democracy a man, through his influence upon the people, wields power alone; but only the ordinary state of things can be at issue here, not the personal influence of some individuals.

The arbitrary authority of a commander over his army does not create the despotism of one man. The bey of Algiers can have the officers of his troops beheaded; but he is obliged to conform to the prejudices, pretensions and whims of the militia.

3

There are two kinds of despotism, which could be called legal and factual if the word "legal" could be applied to despotism, but which I will call direct and indirect despotism. Direct despotism occurs in every country where representatives of the citizens do not exercise the most extensive right of opposition, and do not have adequate means to amend laws they find contrary to reason and justice. Indirect despotism exists when, despite the intent of the law, representation is neither equal nor real, or when one is subjected to an authority that is not established by law.

Thus, in England, for example, one will find that direct despotism exists, since the right of veto of the king and the House of Lords leaves the nation without legal avenues to revoke a bad law,[1] and the representatives of the people only have, in order to obtain such reform, indirect means which are equally offensive to reason, national dignity and public order. But England is above all subjected to indirect despotism, because the House of Commons, which should by law represent the nation, does not in reality represent it; because it is only an aristocratic body the resolutions of which are dictated by forty or fifty people, either ministers, lords, or representatives of the boroughs.[2]

4

These two types of despotism almost always go together. In Turkey, one is subjected to the direct despotism of the sultan and of the body of legal professionals, whom he is obliged, by custom at least, to consult—he even has to obtain their authorization in some cases—and who are the real legislators since they also have the authority to interpret civil laws; but the despotism of the Janissaries is only indirect. It is not by virtue of an explicit law or a time-honored custom that the sultan is obliged to yield to their will. In some countries, the populace of the capital exercises indirect despotism; in some others, the leaders of the nation have made themselves subordinate to financiers; government operations depend upon the ease with which advance funds can be obtained from them; they impose their choice of ministers, and so the people are subject to the despotism of bankers.

All these powers, either direct or indirect, form in various countries a body of citizens whose arbitrary will governs the rest of the nation; and often, in the midst of so many masters, it does not know whom it obeys.

5

A few writers,[3] either in good faith or because they belonged to or hoped to become members of the dominant faction, have honored with the name of liberty the anarchy produced by the discord between the various powers; they have called it balance that sort of inertia for doing good even more than for doing harm to which each of these powers is reduced by their mutual resistance; but it would have been necessary to add then that the nation is the fulcrum bearing the weight of the two opposite powers.

To refute this absurd system, we will limit ourselves to a single reflection: Would a slave with two masters, often divided, cease to be a slave? Would he be happier than with only one master?

6

It is easier to free a nation from direct rather than from indirect despotism; it sees the first and suffers from the second unknowingly, often even while considering those who exercise it as its protectors.

Moreover, the means to prevent direct despotism are much simpler. Let it be impossible to make any law, or impose any tax, without the consent of the representatives of the people; let it be impossible to reject any new law necessary to establish the full enjoyment of the natural rights of man, or any amendment to old laws, if they are called for by the same representatives of the nation or another equally representative body: then direct despotism will be destroyed. In England, as already mentioned, there is no legal way to enact a new law or repeal an old one; the nation only has the indirect means of forcing the other two branches of the legislative power to do so by refusing to consent to other measures; and this is a great flaw which every wise nation should be careful to avoid in its constitution. This flaw does not exist in the United States: their legislative power is divided into several bodies, but several bodies of representatives of the people, which, according to more or less complicated, more or less suitable procedures, have the power to change harmful laws. Thus, direct despotism exists in England, but not in America.

7

Indirect despotism can be exercised by the legislative body itself, the government, certain classes of citizens, church ministers, the legal profession and the courts, the army, financiers, and the populace. We shall describe the ways to prevent these various forms of despotism.

8

Despotism by the legislative body takes place when the representation of the people ceases to be real or becomes too unequal; this danger can be prevented by paying close attention to the composition of laws setting the procedure for electing representatives and the territorial divisions given the right to elect them, and at the same time by making sure the nation has a legal means to change these procedures and divisions, after a fixed period of time, long enough not to make these changes too frequent, but short enough to prevent such development of disorder as would be difficult to eliminate.

9

Despotism by the government will be effectively impeded when the date and length of the assembly of the nation's representatives are made independent of the government's initiative, and when taxes can only be levied with the consent of this assembly. In England, where parliament only meets on the initiative of the king, it has been thought that a remedy to this flaw in the constitution would be found by establishing the custom of consenting to some taxes only for one year. This is not to be imitated; taxes must be set according to the real need of the state, and their duration according to that of the need. But the same goal can be achieved by making each representative assembly responsible, not for the establishment of the tax, but for the order to levy it, deposit it in whichever fund, and arrange provisions for its use. This way, financial operations will have the necessary continuity without resulting in any possible infringement upon freedom.

10

Whenever a certain class of citizens enjoys honorific or pecuniary privileges, and is alone eligible for certain positions opening the only path to all honors and high offices, it is easy to see that this class will become dominant in the representative assembly and that equal representation will subsist in name only. The harm will become much greater if this class of citizens continually recruits new members by admitting all the families that have recently grown rich or have been able to elude the exclusion pronounced against the inferior class. The only cure for such despotism is to let no distinction between citizens remain, either in civil or criminal laws, in their contribution to public expenses, or in their eligibility for offices; so that only inequalities in reputation or wealth would exist, which are in reality neither less natural, nor more unjust, nor more dangerous (if the laws are rational), than inequality in talent and strength. No nation where there is a legally instituted genealogist can be a free nation.

11

The power of the priests is based upon opinion only, and absolute freedom of worship and of the press is its only remedy. In countries steeped in ignorance, this despotism is exercised by the priests themselves; the nation bows down before them: such was their power in Europe until the end of the sixteenth century, when the eyes of the laity began to open. Among enlightened nations, this despotism becomes indistinguishable from that of the populace. Nowhere in Europe, except perhaps in some Swiss republics, is despotism by the clergy alone to be feared, but it becomes so when it is combined with despotism by the aristocracy; this is the case today in the Netherlands, and it was the case in France during the Assembly of Notables.[4]

In countries where there is freedom of religion, the division of the clergy into several sects diminishes its influence; and in countries where the press is free, the populace no longer receives its opinions from priests alone; in addition, the fear of being taken for fools or hypocrites keeps the aristocracy from joining the clergy. One can put forth the example of England as an objection. But,

1. In England, the press is not free in matters of religion.

2. Freedom of worship is not established there.

3. England is in general governed by parties, by associations of accredited people, and these parties carefully foster fanaticism as a tool each hopes to use in turn; therefore, no sooner is it attacked by one of them than the others hasten to its rescue.

12

Despotism by the courts is the most odious of all, because to support and exercise it they use the most respectable tool, the law. In every country where there are permanent courts the members of which are not elected by those under their jurisdiction, and for a limited time only; in every country where civil and criminal justice are joined together, there can be no liberty, because these courts and the commander of the army acting in concert is enough to establish despotism. Such despotism is even more inevitable, if these courts take some part in the legislative power, if they form a body unto themselves, if their members are judged by their own. The commander of the army is then forced to accommodate them, because without them he can only wield absolute power through violence, which is always dangerous. At the same time, their interest lies in flattering or supporting his power, both because they fear him and because they cannot hope that citizens, if they were free, would consent to be subjected to judicial despotism, the necessary consequence of this type of tribunal, because this despotism weighs upon each individual at every moment, and extends to every action, every interest.

If, because of complex laws and procedures, there is a very great number of people associated with the courts who enjoy the exclusive privilege of serving as lawyers or prosecutors, or if it is difficult to replace them, because they are versed in a routine unknown to other citizens, the complete suspension of all justice, which can be caused by obstructionism by the courts or these practitioners, gives judicial despotism a very dangerous strength.

In countries where manners are gentle, despotism by the government, or by the commander of the army, can be neither bloody nor cruel; judicial despotism is always so, because it can unleash the full rigor of the laws, and because courts are careful to maintain stringent laws even when manners have become gentler.

Since the causes of such despotism are known, the cures are easy to see. If judges are periodically elected by the people under their jurisdiction, if civil and criminal courts are kept separate, if judges are expressly compelled to follow the letter of the law, if tribunals of a different order, also elected, are instituted to punish breaches of trust by judges, if there is absolute free access to the function of defending cases before the courts, if private associations that those who fulfill this function would wish to form, instead of being encouraged, are declared contrary to the interests of citizens (for it would be unjust to forbid them), then despotism by the courts will no longer have to be feared.

13

Modern Europeans have found the way to protect themselves from despotism of the army, by dividing it into regiments, distributing it over a great number of garrisons, and not giving permanent commanders to divisions comprising several regiments. Therefore, since the institution of this practice, no army has either disturbed the tranquility of the state, or exercised any despotism, either over the prince, commander of the army, or the citizens. One must except Russia, where the regiments of the guards hold too much sway, and perhaps also Prussia, if in the future the garrison of the royal residence remains very strong and the king is not a military man. The only way to lay European states open to this despotism by the army, to which the other parts of the Old World are subjected, and which impedes the progress of civilization there, would be to make troops loath to obey their leaders passively—obedience which must be limited only by natural right and a positive law—and instill into commanders, officers, and consequently soldiers, the idea that they can make themselves judges of the legitimacy of the orders they receive. Passive obedience is dangerous to public liberty; arbitrary insubordination would become more so. To avoid both of these ills, it is necessary to set by law limits on the military power used to maintain public order and support the enforcement of laws, judgments, and acts of the government. Such a law exists in England: it is a wise institution to be imitated, remembering above all that imitating is not copying.

14

European governments have realized that the impossibility of waging war for a long period of time while relying on the ordinary income of the state or special taxes, would not allow them to indulge in this restless activity which, since the fifteenth century, has become a nearly universal political disease. To compensate for this, governments at first devised the sale of offices, financial agreements involving the temporary alienation of certain rights, and finally direct borrowing. This way, one had the principal at one's disposal, and the interest was paid with taxes or duties. The usefulness of loans would have been very limited if none but the capital meant to be invested in these loans had been available to sell them off, and above all it would have been very slow. But two expedients presented themselves: one was to borrow from finance companies the members of which would thus undertake to advance money or find some within their family, social circle, or among business people connected with them; the other, to sell the loan to bankers or money merchants who would then resell it or speculate on it. These two expedients would be purchased either at the price of higher interest, or in the first case by surrendering some rights, showing more tolerance for some abuses, or even only by shoring up offices the reimbursement of which would be made more difficult by these loans. Then these expedients went beyond all bounds; and unfortunately governments gradually grew accustomed to considering them as certain, to making the success of the most important undertakings dependent upon them, and in difficult circumstances even the interest payments on old loans, and payments required to fulfill obligations or cover public expenses. But from then on the state became subordinate to those who could advance these sums; it became necessary, in legislating taxation or trade, in political dealings, to accommodate their interests, prejudices and passions; and they had to be added to the classes of citizens which exercise a genuine despotism over the people. Thus, in England, they have usurped from the nation the sovereignty of India, which until now has been impossible to take back from them; they caused Mr. Pitt's program, dictated by them, to be preferred to that of Mr. Fox and Earl Stanhope. How many ministers could be named whose fall they brought about or whose appointment they imposed? In France, they forced the government to deprive of his freedom the author of the *Theory of Taxation*,[5] and his birth, wealth and personal reputation could not protect him from their dark hatred. They forced the bankruptcy of 1770 on the

Abbé Terray,[6] who could think only of that solution in order to free himself from their influence, who engaged in many bad transactions to elude it, and ended by giving in to it. The bankruptcy of 1788 had the same cause.

There are only two ways to destroy this despotism, which threatens to become more dangerous and unbearable every day. The first lies in laws which, by banishing all forms of onerous taxes and leaving trade entirely free, would extinguish the source of great fortunes in finance and banking, lower profits in this latter type of commerce, and divide them up into a larger number of hands.[7] The second consists in changing loan procedures by making, when loans have been consented to by the nation, or the assembly representing it, or assemblies representing each province, the nation or such assemblies do the borrowing themselves, pay interest on the loans and reimburse them with funds left in their hands, without any possibility of misappropriation; in seeking, instead of expensive loans requiring only half-hearted confidence, loans that would be attractive only because of well-founded, lasting confidence and the benefits they provide; in attaching to each loan a statement of the real interest rate and a proof that funds meant to pay it off are really sufficient; in always keeping loans available with a rate lower than old loans, to be used to pay them off; in carefully avoiding all financial transactions and all institutions which bring about large stock movements, and along with them, necessarily, associations between business people; finally, in trying to dispel the shadows with which they have obscured a minor art, not at all complicated, that has importance and can become dangerous only to the extent that it remains little known.

15

Despotism by the populace is to be feared in all countries where there are large trading towns and a great capital. But it is less a despotic force in itself than the agent of another power, if we except the power wielded by the populace to force the government to tax goods needed for subsistence and conform to its prejudices in laws regulating trade in these goods. Even then, this despotism only exists because some of the other despotic powers weighing upon a nation, or the various parties sharing these powers, hope to use it to their advantage. In other circumstances, the populace only uses its despotism to support religious prejudices, maintain the authority of specific institutional bodies it has taken under its protection or which enrich such and such town, protect certain popular opinions useful to some classes of citizens and harmful to the rest, and finally, because of animosity towards powerful men it has been taught to hate. However dangerous this despotism may be, nowhere are other powers seen consulting and acting together to destroy it; it is a tool that the weakest want to preserve for themselves. In England, the House of Commons prefers to let stand countless ridiculous and unjust laws, but which the populace would defend, rather than seek the means to destroy this corrupting influence on legislation. The populace deprived Holland of its liberty by reinstituting the office of stadtholder in 1777. Instead of setting right the tyrannical aristocracy of Denmark, the populace introduced there the despotism of the prince, that is to say, the despotism of the court, the priests, and the legal profession. Despotism by the populace of Constantinople destroyed the Greek empire as much as theological disputes and the weapons of the barbarians. We all know that this despotism is as absurd in its projects as it is barbarian in its means, since it is exercised by the most ignorant and corrupt part of each nation, next to the ambitious men who exploit it. But what makes the populace of a large city dangerous? The ease with which it can be assembled, its ignorance and brutality; it is therefore by attacking these three causes that their effects can be prevented.

There are only two ways to reduce the ease with which the populace can be assembled: The first is complete freedom for industry and trade, which from the start would increase the numbers of the people by reducing those of the populace, weaken the private union of workers attached to such and such guild, such and such particular place, finally lessen the aversion that the poorest class, oppressed by the regulations of the guilds, feels for any sort of policing. The second would be to divide each large city into districts, which could assemble for their common interests, following a fixed procedure, and to make the last subdivisions small enough. Small assemblies of citizens who meet without distinction of rank and occupation are in general the only fair way, and at the same time the surest, to prevent spontaneous associations from disturbing public tranquility.

To reduce ignorance, freedom of the press must be restored and well-directed assistance in public education increased.[8] This assistance is lacking in nearly all countries where, run by church ministers, institutions confine themselves to introducing into the mind of the people ideas suited to supporting the power of the clergy. Freedom of the press is another means by which to diminish the ignorance and prejudices of the people, not by educating it directly, but by spreading enlightenment among the closest superior class, and above all by preventing those in whose interest it is to deceive the people from fostering its prejudices. When it rises up, it is seldom in support of its real interests; examples of this could be cited, old and new. Brutality is born out of ignorance, poverty, the harshness of criminal laws, the arrogance of privileged classes; and consequently, one sees how it can be destroyed.

16

These simple observations are enough to show how far those who believe they would really destroy despotism by eliminating arbitrary orders from the government are from knowing the full extent of this scourge. In always speaking of weights to oppose to such despotism, they forget that this despotism itself acts as counterweight to the others, and that, to be consistent, they should wish to see it maintained.

17

One must not mistake tyranny for despotism. Tyranny must be understood as any violation of human rights perpetrated by the law on behalf of public authority. It can exist even independently of despotism. Despotism is the use or abuse of an illegitimate power, a power which does not emanate from the nation or the representatives of the nation; tyranny is the violation of a natural right by a legitimate or illegitimate power.

Let us imagine a very well-ordered republic in the fourteenth, fifteenth, sixteenth, and even the seventeenth century, where the representatives of the people could have opposed the institution of new laws as well as imposed the amendment of old ones; let us suppose that none of the powers set up by these laws could have either violated them or exerted on the representatives of the people a force that would impede their freedom; nevertheless, this republic would have passed penal laws against heretics; what is called sacrilege or blasphemy would have been ranked among capital crimes. In those centuries, and even in this one, trade and industry would have been impeded by restrictive laws. Indirect taxes would have been imposed and crimes created that would have necessitated tyrannical laws to prevent them. There would have been no despotism, tyranny would have been complete.

18

The only way to prevent tyranny, that is to say, the violation of human rights, is to gather all these rights in a declaration, to expound upon them with clarity and in great detail, to publish this declaration with solemnity, ordaining therein that the legislative power, in whatever form it may be established, will not be able to prescribe anything contrary to any of these articles.

At the same time, a legal procedure must be set up, according to which new articles can be added to this declaration, because with the progress of enlightenment men will know the extent of their rights better and will be better able to discern their obvious consequences. The more extensive a declaration of rights, the more certain the enjoyment of those it contains, but also the more the number and complexity of the laws are reduced, and the more those arbitrary provisions which disfigure them among all nations will be seen to disappear. In addition, there must be a legal procedure to strike articles out of this declaration, because error, even in favor of human rights, can be harmful. The procedure to add an article must be such that its addition be assured even if the corresponding right is merely likely to be real; but to strike one out, the procedure must be such that obvious facts and necessity alone can produce a decision in favor of its suppression. Without such a precaution, whatever form is given to the constitution, citizens will not be shielded from tyranny; it will be established by a legitimate power, but it will be no less tyrannical, just as a wrong judgment is no less unjust for having been delivered according to legal procedures.

19

The natural rights of man are:

1. Security and freedom for his person.
2. Security and freedom for his property.
3. Equality.[9]

The last of these rights alone needs an explanation. The type of equality between men required by natural rights excludes any inequality which is not a necessary consequence of the nature of man and things, and which, therefore, would be the arbitrary creation of social institutions. Thus, for example, inequality in wealth is not contrary to natural rights; it is a necessary consequence of the right of property, since this right including the free enjoyment of property, includes therefore the freedom to accumulate it indefinitely. But this inequality would become contrary to natural rights if it were the creation of a positive law, such as the law granting a larger share to the firstborn, the one establishing entails, and so forth. Thus, the sort of superiority a man in charge of an office enjoys over those who are subordinate to him by the nature of this office is not contrary to natural rights, because it is derived from the necessity that some men exercise this authority and others obey it. But this superiority becomes contrary to natural rights if it is made hereditary, or if it extends beyond what is necessary for the duties of the office to be performed well. The right to equality is not infringed upon if only property owners have the right to vote, because they alone own the territory, because their consent alone gives the right to live within it; but it is infringed upon if the right to vote is distributed unequally among various classes of property owners, because such a distinction does not result from the nature of things.[10]

20

The natural rights of man are known in general to all those with a sound mind and a noble soul, but few people take in their full scope, few have risen high enough to discern all the consequences of these rights.

A complete declaration of rights would be a useful work for humankind; but perhaps not a single people could be found, even among those who hate tyranny the most, that could be made to adopt it in its entirety, so much has habit familiarized man with his chains.

21

The first declaration of rights truly worthy of the name is that of Virginia, adopted on June 1, 1776;[11] and the author of this work deserves the everlasting gratitude of humankind.[12] Six other American states have followed the example of Virginia.

But none of these declarations of rights can be regarded as complete.

1. None indicates the limits of sovereign power with respect to the punishment of crimes. But it is obvious that the legislative power does not have the right to make crimes of acts which do not directly, immediately and seriously infringe upon the rights of either an individual or society.

2. None specifies the limits of legislative power with respect to either civil laws or laws for the policing of public order.

3. Only one declares contrary to natural rights any capitation[13] or any tax *on the poor* (expression which reveals deep knowledge on the matter), but none excludes indirect taxes, which, by nature, are unequally apportioned, and cannot exist without violating more or less directly individual freedom or property rights, and without the creation of arbitrary crimes.

4. While some proscribe any exclusive privilege, none ranks among natural and sacred rights the freedom every man must retain to use his abilities and property as he pleases, as long as he does not prejudice the rights of others; a freedom which implies complete freedom for industry and trade.

5. Some allow the imposition of taxes to pay for church expenses, applicable, it is true, to any denomination according to the will of the taxpayer; but any tax of this kind is contrary to the rights of men, who must remain free not to support, or attend, any church.

6. They generally include the right not to be convicted except by a unanimous jury. But it has not been demonstrated (1) that this unanimity, required according to English procedure, gives a greater probability of reaching a correct judgment than a direct majority of eight or ten judges. (2) It has not been demonstrated either that jurors are more trustworthy judges of fact than men chosen by the citizens from among those who enjoy the best reputation for knowledge and integrity, and chosen to serve in this capacity for a certain period of time.

The choice between these various methods is not a matter of rights but a matter of reasoning. The legislative power must have the authority to establish the procedure it deems best suited to uphold personal security, and a declaration of rights must exclude what would be contrary to them and not prescribe a choice between the various means which uphold them equally.

Thus, for example, any nomination of judges or jurors other than by popular election, any creation of a self-recruiting permanent court, or a court appointed by a body of citizens or a supreme magistrate, and so forth, must be proscribed by a declaration of rights.

7. In several of these declarations, those who, as a matter of conscience, do not believe themselves allowed to bear arms are exempted from forced military service. This is a privilege granted to people holding a particular opinion, and therefore a violation of a general right. The principle leading to respecting individual conscience in what would really fall within the province of the laws is just an inducement to fanaticism. It would not be fair to force into service a man needed by his family, and exempt from it a Quaker or a member of another sect. But a general exemption from any forced military service must be part of a declaration of rights. The call to service must be free, and the punishment for refusal is the shame attached to cowardice everywhere. Thus, opinion alone would decide on the legitimacy of the reason for refusal.

22

The best way to procure a complete declaration of rights would be to encourage enlightened men to each draw up, separately, a model for one. By comparing these various works, one could not only assess the more or less methodical order in which rights are presented, or the clarity of style; but one would also know everything these various citizens consider to be included under human rights, and this would be the surest way to know them all, perhaps not in their true and absolute scope, but that to which the current state of knowledge allows them to be extended.

Each drafter would confine himself to explaining rights with simple reasons, expressed in few words, as is the case in the Virginia declaration. But, regarding rights which can be considered questionable, they could, in separate notes, enter into more extensive discussion.

The difficulty of recognizing every human right, of explaining them with clarity and method, is not the only one faced by a work of this kind; it must be composed in such a way that, while avoiding verbosity and minute details, each right is explained so as to make any serious violation of it obvious and susceptible of a simple demonstration within the reach of all minds.

It would also be necessary to carefully separate the essential part of each article, in which a right is stated, from the reasons which cause it to be considered as within the natural rights of man. Finally, this presentation should be such that, after having drawn up, by comparing these various sketches, a complete list of all that is considered part of these rights, a large assembly could decide by an up or down vote which of them it thinks must be included in a declaration of rights, and which it deems either illusory or exaggerated.

It would be desirable to make these sketches public by way of the printed word; in this, there would be a double advantage, that of submitting them to the criticism of all citizens and benefitting from the enlightenment that can result, and that of being able to say that the nation has not neglected to examine any of the rights that any single member of the state could have wanted to claim, since it would then be by his own doing (given this publicity) that a right believed by him to be real would not have been submitted for discussion.

The more extensive and complete a declaration of rights, the clearer and more precise, the more certain to be protected from all tyranny will be the nation that has adopted it, that is attached to it by principle and opinion; for any tyranny that obviously attacks one of these rights would see a general opposition rise against it.

23

Another benefit of a declaration of rights is to guarantee public tranquility: a nation armed with this shield ceases to be suspicious of every innovation, can no longer allege any pretext for taking offence at useful changes, no longer allows itself to be so easily deceived by defenders of abuses it wants to destroy, no longer mistakes for its rights privileges contrary to these very rights and institutions opposed to its interests. Have we not seen the people of the Netherlands rise up to support a few seminaries or convents? Other countries regard as part of their liberties, here the preservation of a tyrannical aristocracy, there a court system incompatible with the enjoyment of their true rights? A declaration of rights is therefore the safeguard of both public tranquility and freedom.[14]

Eulogy of Franklin:
Read at the Public Session of the Academy of Sciences, November 13, 1790 (1790)

Eripuit cœlo fulmen, mox sceptra Tyrannis.

—*Turgot, 1775*

Benjamin Franklin was born in Boston on January 6, 1706, the son of Josiah Franklin and Abiah Folger.[1]

His father had settled in Boston around 1682; attached to the Presbyterian religion by a hereditary zeal, he had left England, where it was only tolerated, to seek a country where it would be free.

Attacks against the independence of religious opinions have revived the spirit of liberty in Europe and peopled America. Persecution forced men to finally recognize their true rights, hardly known even in ancient republics, and the human race owed its liberation and enlightenment to what had only been invented to make its enslavement and degradation complete.

Josiah Franklin had had fifteen children[2] with two wives. Benjamin was the last son. His natural inclination for reading caused him to be destined for the clergy. But his father could not afford the expense of such an education,[i] and the young Franklin, forced to seek a mechanical profession, chose an apprenticeship in his elder brother's print shop. He was fifteen years old when chance presented him with an odd volume of the *Spectator*.[3] Delighted with the philosophy and style of this work, he decided to take it as a model; he would choose a topic in it, write down the main ideas, then try to discuss the subject and compare his work with that of the master he had thus given himself. Through this exercise, to which he could only devote himself at the expense of time intended for sleep or rest, he soon acquired enough practice to dare to also write articles like those in the *Spectator*. His

---

i. At first a dyer, he had become a candle maker; but, in a country where ownership of the land, available to anyone who wished to farm it, seemed to call every inhabitant to this first occupation of civilized man, and where the independent life it provides was the greatest good and the object of all work, the scarcity of craftsmen, and the resulting high level of wages, left manufacturers the hope of only uncertain and limited success.

brother published a gazette; he sent him his first attempts, hiding his name and disguising his handwriting; they were read in front of their gathered friends, and Mr. Franklin enjoyed the pleasure of hearing them applauded, and of seeing that their author was being looked for among the most famous writers doing honor to the still-emerging literature of New England. He could not keep his secret for very long, and by revealing it became an object of esteem and almost admiration in his small social circle; but his brother, naturally haughty, deemed that a young man of seventeen, who was an author, would not be a very docile printer's boy. Soon afterwards, his temper forced Mr. Franklin to leave him. He left his family, went to New York, where he could not find any work, left for Philadelphia and arrived, with only two shillings as his entire fortune, in this city of which he was destined to become the legislator, and from which he would sail away fifty years later entrusted with the destiny of two worlds.

After a very short stay in Philadelphia, he set sail for London, misled by the governor of Pennsylvania, who had promised him the means to acquire the types and presses necessary to set up a printing shop in America. Once in England, he found himself with no other resource than his craft, which, for him, was still only a trade. But he had understood early the benefits of sobriety and work. He had grown accustomed to a thrifty but healthy diet, suitable to sustain his strength, but keeping his mind entirely free. What an English worker earned was plenty for an American philosopher, and gave him the opportunity to devote part of his time and wages to his education.

He read then the works of Collins[4] and Shaftesbury, and they inspired in him the principles of that skepticism which, in the Greek schools, had degenerated into a ridiculous charlatanism, but which, among the moderns, freed from those pedantic subtleties, became the true philosophy; and which consists, not in doubting everything, but in weighing all the evidence by submitting it to rigorous analysis; not in proving that man cannot know anything, but in carefully discerning and choosing as the object of his curiosity what it is possible to know.

Palmer, in whose shop Mr. Franklin was working, was then printing *The Religion of Nature Delineated* by Wollaston.[5] The young student, unhappy with the principles of this work, tried to refute some of them and published a small *Dissertation on Liberty and Necessity, Pleasure and Pain*.

Soon, his inclination for philosophy, zeal for study, appealing naïveté and wisdom beyond his years caused him to be admitted into the social circles of several men who were very famous at the time, Mandeville,[6] Lyons,[7] Pemberton[8] and Hans Sloane.[9]

Soon after his return to America, two of his friends, Messrs. William Coleman and Robert Grace, advanced him the funds to buy a printing shop. Undoubtedly, their names deserve to be remembered with gratitude; they gave back to their country a great man that nature had formed, but necessity could have stolen. The history of science is full of such examples; it often shows us genius struggling against adversity; and, through the example of those whom chance has allowed to triumph over it, it makes apparent everything humankind has lost, and what it could hope for from a type of public institution which, securing for the first glimmers of talent the means to get noticed, would then provide those to reach as high as nature allowed it to aspire.

In England, Mr. Franklin had observed the benefits of paper gazettes, of associations known as clubs, and of voluntary subscriptions; he decided to help his own country enjoy the same. First he published a gazette[10] which he would fill out, when news was lacking, with pieces in which moral lessons were almost always presented in the form of apologues; where reason was enlivened by naïve and gentle jesting; where philosophy, while remaining within the reach of simple men for whom it was intended, was at the same level as in Europe. It was the *Spectator*, but more natural, with more simplicity and grace, with a larger and above all more useful purpose. Instead of entertaining the uncertain hope of curing of some of its vices a people corrupted by wealth and inequality, it aspired to reform the ideas, refine and magnify the virtues of an emerging nation. Several of the pieces published by Mr. Franklin at that time have been preserved, and there are some that Voltaire and Montesquieu would not have disavowed.

He never allowed this gazette to be sullied by personal attacks. This easy method of directing public hatred towards those one wishes to harm seemed to him as vile as it was dangerous. He only saw it as a treacherous weapon skillfully used by hypocrites and agitators to cast suspicion on talents and virtues, render all reputations uncertain, destroy the authority of a good name—a guide so necessary to a still hardly enlightened people who is preparing itself for or awakening to newfound freedom—and thus hand over public trust to shady intriguers who will know how to take advantage of it.

At the same time, he was publishing an almanac he sought to make useful by filling in empty spaces on the pages with a small number of precepts.

He would include in it advice on thrift, lessons on charity and justice suitable to guide the conduct of a simple and laborious life; and he was careful to end them with a common proverb, in order to impress them more surely in the reader's memory. This almanac was meant above all for those who, living in the far corners of the colony, absorbed by work and domestic cares, hardly had other occasions to read. He wanted no class of citizen to remain without education, none to be doomed to receive only false ideas from books intended to pander to its credulity or feed its prejudices. A simple printer was then doing for America what the wisest governments had neglected through pride, or feared to do out of weakness. He has since gathered all these lessons in the work that is so famous under the title *Poor Richard's Almanack*, unparalleled model, in which one cannot help but recognize a superior man without being able to cite a single stroke through which he reveals himself. Nothing in the thoughts or style is above the least-trained intelligence; but philosophy easily discovers in it subtle views and profound intentions. His expression is always natural, often commonplace even, and all the refinement is in the choice of ideas. To make his lessons more useful, he does not notify his readers that a learned man from the city is willing to stoop so low as to educate them, and he hides behind the name of Poor Richard, as ignorant and poor as they are.

Americans were not then that nation of philosophers which, by the wisdom of its institutions, has since astonished Europe. Religion and the work required to settle a wild country had been the only occupations of the first generations of Europeans. Mr. Franklin saw how much they needed the light of philosophy; but they had to be made aware of this without declaring an intention which would have advertised its superiority. He formed a club among those of the inhabitants of Philadelphia whose station in life was close to his. It consisted of only twelve people, and their number was never increased. However, prompted by his advice, most members soon set up other similar associations. This way, he made sure that they would be animated by the same spirit. But he was careful not to link them together formally, and even more so not to make them subordinate to the first association. He wanted to establish a more intimate communication of knowledge and opinions between citizens, make them grow accustomed to consulting together for their common interests, and not spread his own ideas or create a party for himself. He believed that while a private association must never hide, it must still less show itself; while it is useful when it acts through the separate influence of its members, through the concurrence of their intentions and the weight their virtues or talents lend to their opinions, it can become dangerous if, acting as a whole and forming as it were a nation within the nation, it manages to create a public will different from the people's and to place between individuals and national sovereignty a foreign power which, led by an ambitious rascal, would threaten freedom as well as the laws.[11]

It is customary in English clubs to impose a small fine on those who stray from the rules of the association. In Franklin's club in Philadelphia, one would pay a fine whenever one indulged in harsh words. The men most intrepid in their self-assurance were forced to use expressions of doubt, and to grow accustomed in their speech to a modesty which, even if it did not extend beyond words, would already procure the benefit of not hurting the feelings of others, but which, through the very powerful influence of words upon ideas, necessarily ends up extending to opinions themselves.[ii]

At the same time, Mr. Franklin was skillfully waging war against fanaticism, which was bound to have grown deep roots in a country peopled by persecution. Those feelings of universal benevolence, which find their way so easily into gentle and pure souls, those maxims of simple truth, which good sense does not reject when it is not corrupted by a false doctrine, led little by little to leniency and reason, and at least made powerless for harm an enemy it would have been imprudent to attack openly. Thus, during the same period, in the two hemispheres, philosophy was avenging the human race against the tyrant who had long oppressed and degraded it; but it was fighting with different weapons. In one, fanaticism was an error by individuals, the unfortunate fruit of their education and readings. It was enough to enlighten them, to dispel the ghosts of a wild imagination. It was above all the fanatics themselves who needed to be cured. In the other, where fanaticism, guided by politics, had created a system of oppression based upon error, where, linked to every kind of tyranny, it had promised them to blind humankind so that they would allow it to oppress men, it was necessary to rouse public opinion and for the friends of reason and freedom to join forces against a dangerous power. It was not a question of enlightening fanatics, but of unmasking and disarming them. It can be added to this parallel unique in the history of philosophy, that the two men who had separately

ii. To declare not to harbor any feeling of animosity against any club member.
To profess an equal affection for all men, whatever their creed.
To regard as an act of tyranny any infringement upon freedom of worship or opinion.
To love truth for itself, to try to know it, to take pleasure in hearing it, to strive to spread it.
Such was the profession of faith of this club, which was of great service to the national assemblies of Pennsylvania, and never claimed to rule them.

formed this beneficial plan, Voltaire and Franklin, were able to meet in Paris in their old age, revel together in their glory, and take satisfaction in their triumph.

Encouraged by the trust of his fellow citizens, Mr. Franklin believed he could envision plans more difficult to carry out, but more directly useful. By means of open subscriptions that he proposed, and in which, thanks to the wisdom of his plans, everyone was eager to participate, Philadelphia acquired a public library, a hospital, a fire insurance company, a college and soon an academy. When he would put forth a project for an institution, he would carefully avoid claiming the idea for himself. Experience had demonstrated to him how important it is, to achieve success, not to let the pettiness of vanity compete with the zeal for public good. Any man who wants to influence opinion walks between enthusiasm and envy; and knowing how difficult it is to sustain enthusiasm, or control it, he would rather disarm envy, even at the expense of his glory.

He had invented for himself a method by which one could hope to improve oneself by means of a small number of rules the daily observation of which was meant to destroy imperceptibly those habits of weakness and passions that are detrimental to happiness and degrade morals, and then give wisdom and virtue all the strength of a natural inclination. He knew that thrift, regular work, and a simple life, by contributing to personal happiness, remove the interest or temptation to disturb the happiness of others, and that the resulting peace of the soul makes virtues easy to practice. He had observed that he who, in his everyday conduct, indifferent to good or evil, surrenders to the power of circumstances and customs, cannot be sure of himself in moments when his duties impose sacrifices upon him. Like intelligence, the soul perfects itself, becomes stronger, and refines itself by continual exercise. But the general system of beings opens up an immeasurable prospect to the mind, where it can move freely, vary its efforts, where its activity finds ever renewed, ever inexhaustible nourishment. The exercise of moral faculties, on the contrary, is subjected to the events and circumstances of each day, and a kind of art is needed to have emerge out of this the means to develop and extend these faculties, to increase their energy.

From these precepts, suitable to improve the individual who would adopt them as a rule of conduct, Mr. Franklin soon rose to the idea of an institution intended for the moral improvement of the human race. He had formed the plan of an association extending all over the world, each member of which would make it the special object of his life and work. It was to consist of young people, whose soul is purer, more flexible, and capable of more effort, and whose emerging reason can combine with docility and enthusiasm without getting weaker and going astray. This was the project Pythagoras had conceived, and even realized, more than two thousand years ago, but with opposite means. The Greek philosopher wanted, by force of habit, to substitute for natural feelings and impulsions the principles he thought necessary to inspire in men; the American philosopher only wished to refine, strengthen and channel the movements of nature. One had intended to enslave and transform man, the other only aspired to enlighten and improve him. One had devised a system which could, in one nation, at a given time, produce a happy revolution, stun the people with great virtues, and which soon was to exist only in their memory, destroyed by the irresistible force of nature the laws of which he had run counter to. The means of the other, in keeping with these laws, suited to all countries as well as all times, worked toward a slow but lasting improvement; and without making any century glorious, could contribute to the happiness of all.

But the philosopher who was preparing the felicity of his country by enlightening men to form citizens was destined to be of more direct and no less useful service to it. Time was no more when the poverty of the English colonies was enough to prevent the wars of Europe from reaching them. Already they could tempt the greed of an enemy, and it was becoming equally dangerous for their tranquility and freedom to be either abandoned by Great Britain or defended by its soldiers. Mr. Franklin, who had been clerk of the Pennsylvania assembly since 1736, judged it necessary to take advantage of a time of war when it was in England's interest to allow Pennsylvanians to take up, for the defense of their territory, the same arms which would one day become needed against itself in order to uphold their rights; and in 1744,[12] he conceived the plan of a national militia. The people accepted it. Ten thousand men were armed, Philadelphia alone supplied a thousand. Mr. Franklin was asked to assume their command, he refused, and served as a soldier under Mr. Lawrence, whom he had himself proposed as general. Forts needed to be built, and money was lacking; he provided for this through a lottery of his own invention.

The success of these measures faced a singular difficulty. Quakers are in great number in Pennsylvania; and in the purity of the principles of their sect, they consider it a sin to contribute, even with their money, to a defensive war. The natural consequence of overly strict moral precepts, adopted under the influence of religious enthusiasm, is to make it necessary for their followers to either violate them, or sacrifice to them the counsel of reason and the sentiments of natural moral law. Then, they seek to evade their own laws, they hide their violation with subtle distinctions, skillful ambiguities. This way, they avoid rousing against themselves the fanatics or hypocrites of their sect, and they do not offend the populace who, in all religions, relates its moral notions only to sanctioned expressions.[iii]

Mr. Franklin's philosophical indulgence, and his shrewdness of mind, often helped him reconcile the patriotism of the Quakers with the proprieties of their sect.

Never has a man of such elevated mind, such independent soul, known how to respect more scrupulously the religious weaknesses and the pettiness of a misled conscience; he would display for weak and sickly minds those delicate attentions, those refinements in solicitude, which men of ordinary benevolence show for infirmity and childhood.

Mr. Franklin's education had not opened up for him a career in the sciences, but nature had given him a genius for them. His first attempts regarding electricity reveal that he knew very little even on that part of physics. Far from Europe, he had only imperfect experimental tools. However, he soon surmised the immediate cause of electrical phenomena. He explains them by the presence of a fluid, imperceptible as long as it stays in balance, and which manifests itself, either when this balance is upset, or as it is being restored. His analysis of the Leyden jar is a masterpiece of sagacity, accuracy and subtlety all at once. The varied and almost fantastic phenomena it offers depend on a single fact, the electrical difference existing between the two isolated surfaces of an idioelectrical body, and the instantaneous return to equilibrium when contact is established between them.

Soon after, he notices a striking analogy between the effects of lightning and those of electricity. He invents a device with which he proposes to examine the sky; the experiment is tried, and the outcome confirms his conjectures. Thus, the cause of lightning is known. Its effects, which are so varied, so strange in appearance, are not only explained but reproduced, the only truly demonstrative proof of theories which are not yet reduced to calculated

---

iii. Thus the Quakers, asked to grant a sum of money that was needed to buy powder, gave some to buy wheat, rye and other grains.

Thus the Dunkers, wiser than the Quakers, have always refused to sanction by public formulae either their dogmas or their precepts. They were afraid, as one of their leaders told Mr. Franklin one day, they would lay themselves open to the danger of professing what they no longer believed, or to the shame of changing their mind.

laws. We finally understand why lightning travels peacefully along certain bodies, and shatters others so violently; why it melts metals, and sometimes smashes to pieces or sometimes seems to respect substances around them. But being able to imitate lightning was a small achievement. Mr. Franklin conceives the audacious idea of diverting its blows. He observed that a pointed rod, by slowly restoring balance between differently charged masses, even at a distance where soft materials would exert no action, would stop or reduce the volume of sparks, and would weaken or eliminate all phenomena. He imagines that a pointed iron bar, the base of which by joining with the moist ground could create contact between a cloud and the earth, would prevent the explosion of lightning, and protect objects near the conductor. His expectation is met with success, and man holds in his hands the power to disarm the sky.

New experiments on pointed rods reveal to him every secret of their operation, the laws and limits of their influence. How to protect objects from lightning becomes an exact art with its methods and rules.

This discovery was too brilliant and original not to unite against it the many enemies of everything that challenges ordinary ideas. However, America and England at once adopted the use of conductors. But at the beginning of the rift between the two, English physicists were seen seeking, with misleading experiments, to cast doubt on the utility of these techniques, and trying to rob Mr. Franklin of his discovery to punish him for having caused them to lose thirteen provinces.

It is unfortunately easier to mislead a nation on the subject of its interests than to deceive scientists on an experiment; and the same influence which could lead the English into an unjust and ill-fated war, could not succeed in changing the form of electrical conductors. They grew more numerous in France when it became America's ally; in truth, police decrees were issued against them in some towns, as had been done in Italy with decisions by casuists, but with as little success. In free countries, laws follow public opinion; in others, public authority often runs counter to it, but ends by yielding submissively to its influence. Today, the use of this preventive tool has become widespread among nearly all nations, but without being general. A long series of experiments no longer allows any doubt regarding its effectiveness. If buildings equipped with it still have some dangers to fear, it is because only an unequal struggle can ever take place between the efforts of man, always so limited, and the forces of nature. But what immeasurable prospect does this success not open up to our hopes? Why would the deadly activity of every scourge not be seen to yield some day, like that of lightning, to the power of genius applying itself over the vastness of centuries, and all the rigors of nature disarmed by a successful use of its gifts, not leave us to experience only its blessings?

The Royal Society of London, to which Mr. Franklin's first attempts had been presented, neglected them for several years. It was not supposed that an American could teach anything to the physicists of Europe, and that a man unknown in the sciences could, as early as with his first steps, make brilliant discoveries; it was thought better to regard them as illusions. But because of the reputation they were enjoying in France, the Royal Society woke up; and by making Mr. Franklin one of its members, without his solicitation, it showed that it could be just even when it had started out by not being so.

In 1754, Mr. Franklin, who had been a member of the Pennsylvania assembly for two years, was entrusted with negotiating with the savages. This negotiation was to be successful; like him, they spoke only one language, that of common sense and good faith.

These men, whom Europeans have been able to corrupt but not civilize, had long been the object of his curiosity and observations. By comparing them with European nations, he saw to what extent the progress of society had weakened man's physical faculties and increased his intelligence; how social institutions had sometimes corrupted, and sometimes perfected us; what we owed them in terms of virtues and vices; at what immense distance the wonders of the arts, the discoveries in the sciences and the efforts of reason placed us from these men close to nature; whereas, if we weighed in the balance only our progress toward freedom, happiness and virtue, we would find very slight the benefits we have purchased with that long series of crimes and misfortunes that have accompanied our course, until now so uncertain and troubled. By comparing the life of the savage to that of country folk, he found that we have done much for the class of men to whom enlightenment is not alien, but still very little for the majority of the human race; and that, while the man who is virtuous and uses his reason is superior to the inhabitant of the forests of Ohio, ordinary people have often simply substituted degrading vices for the brutality of the savage, and prejudices for his ignorance.

More than once in his works he took pleasure in setting the naïve good sense of the Indians against the proud reason of civilized men, and their unfailing calm and profound indifference, against the passions which trouble us for imaginary interests. He seemed to think that the savage was less different than most of us from what man perfected by reason, without ceasing to be subject to nature, would be.

In 1754, the king of England, who had planned to attack France, called together a general congress of deputies from the various colonies to consult on a system of common defense. Mr. Franklin was sent to it, and proposed a plan for their union which was accepted by the congress; but neither the particular assemblies of each state, nor the British government, liked it. No threat had yet made the colonies feel the need for this union, which was to take away from each some part of its independence; and the English government was both too skilled not to foresee what this new institution would prepare in terms of resistance to its own tyrannical undertakings, and not enlightened enough to know that its only remaining power was that of guiding a revolution, the unavoidable consequence of the ever-growing prosperity of the colonies. Indolence or pride on one side, treachery on the other, caused the rejection of a plan inspired by foresight and drawn up by wisdom. Twenty-four years later, it was used as a foundation by the congress which declared independence; and perhaps it would have been desirable for the new constitution to imitate its wise simplicity more. Mr. Franklin was criticized for having granted in this plan a right of veto to a governor appointed by the king of Great Britain; but circumstances required it, it was the bond which was to join together an offshoot, still weak, and the tree from which it had grown, and which needed to be cut only when the young plant, after having grown its roots and extended its branches, had become strong enough to grow and support itself on its own.

We shall not praise Mr. Franklin for having foreseen a revolution to which everything pointed, but for having sought the means with which to spare England and America the misfortunes it was to cost them, and for having wanted it to be the work of reason, and not of force. Convinced that one ought to enlighten men in order to teach them how to conduct themselves, and not excite their passions in order to govern them; that good would always prevail in the end; and that true skill consisted in knowing how to wait for it, in sometimes preparing it, and above all in eliminating obstacles in its path; he abhorred that restless and bloody political practice, which prides itself on building the edifice of public felicity upon ruins, and takes pleasure in surrounding the altar of liberty with victims.

War soon broke out between France and England.[13] The borders of the colonies the two nations then had in America were its apparent cause, and perhaps the British government was already seeking in it a means to distract the Americans with a preoccupation for their safety, and prevent them from thinking too much about the interest they had in rising, by their union, to an independent existence.

In 1755, Mr. Franklin was put in charge of defending the northwest borders of Pennsylvania. He had forts built; he sent help to General Braddock, and sacrificed in this part of his wealth.

This war was successful; but it enlightened the Americans about their strength. They could not hide from themselves the fact that the conquest of Canada had been their doing.

Peace, by securing this vast country for the British Empire, freed them from the fear of a foreign enemy subjected to an absolute government.[iv]

At the same time, England, struck by the rapid growth of the population and wealth of these same colonies, believed it should no longer defer securing the means to make their wealth an instrument of its power. Half a century earlier, any attempt to subject them to taxation could have dissolved these emerging societies; later, they would have acquired enough strength to refuse it. The question was not so much the proceeds of taxation, as it was establishing the right to impose it. Was it to be feared that a small tax, equal to far less than the cost of preparations for defense, would rouse peaceful men, whose customs, needs, kinship and trade relations tied them to the mother country? Thus, an act of parliament imposed a stamp tax[14] and a few taxes on goods upon the American colonies.

Americans had always been free. They were governed by English laws, but these laws were those of their ancestors. They had not received them, but they had brought them along with them; and yet, what is most contrary to civil liberty in these laws had been naturally eliminated, and Americans had been unwilling to tolerate either those remnants of feudalism, or those infringements upon the right to make free use of one's industry, which disgrace English legislation. Their charters protected them from all the violence of arbitrary power. No tax could be collected from them without

---

iv. The Jesuits had not yet been suppressed at the time Canada belonged to France. Their influence on the savages was much dreaded; it was feared that they would manage to turn them into soldiers of the Inquisition. French laws were still the same laws of Louis XIV [the revocation of the Edict of Nantes by Louis XIV in 1685 had ended religious tolerance for Protestants in France], so odious to protestant Europe; people on the other side of the Atlantic Ocean were not aware of the rapid change in public opinion which, foretelling the repeal of these laws, tempered in advance their enforcement; and perhaps this fear of the French would have been enough to counterbalance for a long time, in the English colonies, the desire to break their chains, and to possibly make them bear new ones.

their consent. Strict equality among men, and far greater religious freedom, made them in fact freer than the English. The necessity of obtaining, for their particular laws, the assent of a governor sent from England, and a prohibition on direct trade with foreigners, were the only signs of their dependence. Therefore, it was not for them a question of conquering their freedom, but of defending it, not of recovering rights that had been usurped from them, but of maintaining these rights.[v]

Men farming homesteads spread over a vast expanse of land, or engaged in trade and fishing in a few seaports, whose sole pleasures were reading, hunting, and hospitality, who sought their happiness in the practice of domestic virtues, for whom a meal around which a few friends gathered was a feast, almost all of whom enjoyed that abundance of necessities that is so preferable to the luster of luxury, and hardly knew artificial needs, such men had to be difficult to stir; but steadfast in their resistance, they would bear patiently constraints mitigated by habit, but reject new shackles with horror. Thus, the Stamp Act aroused a general indignation; but remaining calm in this indignation, prompted by sentiments too reasonable to be vented with vain fury, they confined themselves, while asking for the repeal of an unjust law, to declaring their unwavering resolution never to abide by it. Mr. Franklin was entrusted with conveying to London the wishes of Pennsylvania.

More than two years earlier, the king of England had granted him the office of postmaster general of North America.[15] An ordinary man could have thought himself obliged to choose between the duties of gratitude or patriotism. Mr. Franklin believed he had only one to perform, that of telling ministers and the British parliament the truth, as he had done with the citizens of Philadelphia.

The king and the two nations had in his eyes only one and the same interest; and by defending the cause of America, he believed he served England. Such is the simple explanation for his conduct.

In 1766, the House of Commons wished to question and hear him. It was no doubt a fine sight to see the deputy of the free citizens of America defend justice and eternal natural rights in front of men who, also claiming to be the representatives of a free people, could not, without betraying their duty, fail to regard the same freedom as an equal and inalienable possession

---

v. What was at stake, above all, was preserving this maxim, that no one can be subjected to a tax to which their representatives have not consented, and they had received this maxim from England itself, where it was considered sacred; it had been the main cause of the insurrection against Charles I, and the revolution of 1688 had confirmed it.

of all humankind; to hear him, setting the simplicity of courage and reason against the pride of wealth and power, declare that Americans could neither be misled, nor intimidated, nor defeated, and prove it by his countenance and example; showing the English the dangers their policy and power would inevitably bring on; revealing to them the secret of America's strength, without hiding that of its weakness, and speaking to this council of enemy kings as openly as if confiding his opinions and conjectures freely and trustingly to a friend. The power of truth prevailed this time over that of the ministry; the House of Commons was carried along by public opinion, and the Stamp Act was repealed.[vi] But the ministers, persisting in judging the people of America by those of Europe, did not believe it could imperil itself and endure sacrifices in order to frustrate their policy. They recognized the impossibility of instituting a tax in the interior of the country; but they thought it possible to have one tolerated provided it were collected in the ports, and were confident that, in the end, what was already paid in England as export duty would be paid peacefully in America as import duty; for they had been able to reduce the treacherous modesty of their pretentions to this difference alone. Therefore, only a small duty on tea brought to America remained from the original plan.[vii]

It did not occur to the Americans to rebel against this insidious tyranny, and they were satisfied with the resolution to do without tea, and even to forego English goods. The ministers did not think that such a resolution could be serious. They sent tea to Boston. For some time the governors had been wearying the peaceful, but firm, character of the Americans with small vexations, and they did not know how menacing the long patience of a people that is neither corrupt, nor degraded, can be. It is a struggle between reason and courage, and at the moment it stops an irresistible force is released. Some inhabitants of Boston, from the least enlightened class, the least prepared by education to repress the first movements of passion, rose up and

---

vi. This tax is flawed in itself. Everywhere, it is the enemy of commerce and free contracts. But in America, customs, the sparseness of the population, made it more onerous still. Ministers had been wrong even in the choice of their means, and unfortunately for England, they thought this was the only mistake they had made.

vii. This was doubly imprudent; for Americans were thereby made aware that the exclusive privilege on trade included a sure means, albeit indirect, to subject them arbitrarily to taxation, and this yoke they were still bearing with patience became detestable to them. But on the other hand, the debate on the right to tax had to be linked to the interest in maintaining this privilege, which in its mercantilist prejudices England considered one of the main sources of its wealth, so that the English people could see without emotion ministers use violence against the colonies.

burned the tea. English ministers believed a forceful reaction would spread terror. Boston's harbor was closed, and Great Britain lost America forever. Mr. Franklin had remained in Europe all that time. Five of the colonies had successively entrusted him with their interests.

Ministers would sometimes call him to consult him. They considered anyone who did not share their opinion an enemy of England. This was tantamount to announcing that they wished to be misled, and the governors of the colonies had understood them all too well. Nevertheless, Mr. Franklin alone, faithful to his policy, kept telling them the truth. Thus, not satisfied with depriving him of a position in America, where already they no longer had the power to replace him, they stopped paying his emoluments as deputy; finally, they initiated unfair court proceedings against him. In a free country, these lawsuits are the ministers' lettres de cachet,[16] and a few years earlier they had taken vengeance upon Wilkes[17] in the same way.[viii]

Mr. Franklin's trial did not have very serious consequences; a pretext to convict him could not be found in any law, and ministerial vengeance only resulted in having insults publicly said to him by a lawyer whose obliging character has since then been rewarded by the honors of peerage.

Mr. Franklin left England, leaving ministers who were determined to use force and certain to carry the bulk of the nation along for fear of losing the trade with the colonies, and he found America resolved to defend itself. Already, a general congress, consisting of deputies of the various states, was debating how to resist. The states had not had time to decide either how much independence they wanted to preserve, or how much they should give up. They would even have been afraid to disturb their emerging union by discussing this difficult question, and with noble wisdom left it to the moderation of their deputies and to the zeal of each state for the common good. As early as the day after he arrived, Mr. Franklin became a member of Congress.

But in breaking away from England, the colonies remained without a constitution, without a government, and their enemies had rested their hopes in part on the consequences of this anarchy.

---

viii. Ministers' interest in retaining these tools of indirect oppression is one of the main impediments to the improvement of English laws.

Criminal laws which are vague or punish acts harmless in themselves, civil laws which are obscure and applied by courts which, because of their constitution or their weakness, are not protected from outside influence, constitute tools which indolence or corruption too often leave in the hands of despotism, and any nation wishing to remain truly free must hasten to remove them.

They were once again mistaken; they did not understand the wisdom of this people or its noble confidence in its enlightened leadership. Used to the subtleties of old politics, corrupted by the pride of wealthy nations, they could not believe that in the forests of the New World there were men who had thoroughly studied the principles of society, and who, with their earliest endeavors, would give lessons to Europe. To be sure, we should not conclude from this that the Americans were more enlightened than we were; but men easily come to an agreement when a gentle equality has preserved them from the sophisms of interest and vanity; truth is easy to find for an emerging nation free of prejudices, and it is principally to counter the systematic errors of habit and corruption that old nations need all the resources of education, all the powers of genius.

In each colony, the task of drawing up a constitution was entrusted to an assembly given the name of "convention," and made distinct from the assembly which was to exercise legislative power. Nearly everywhere a time limit was set after which these constitutions could be changed by means of a power specifically delegated by the nation for this purpose. In some states, such power was to be granted only to a body entirely distinct from the legislature; in others, investing the representatives with this extraordinary authority when they were elected was enough. Thus, for the first time, it was possible to avoid both the shortcomings of an unstable constitution handed over to the interests of those who are to wield its powers, and those of a permanent constitution which, cut off from the changes and progress of the human race, contains for this reason alone the seed of every evil. Indeed, would not progress itself become dangerous, if it could be misused to take advantage of the flaws of an established constitution but not used to amend it?

Everywhere, religious freedom was respected, and in several states, religion, restored to its natural dignity, was no longer reduced to a mere political institution. In a majority, a declaration of human rights set limits, imposed by nature and justice, on the powers of society; a sublime ideal, of which old covenants between peoples and kings were only crude sketches,[ix] and of which France was to give the Old World the first example. Finally, an absolute prohibition of all hereditary inequalities, both sanctioned as a natural right and stipulated as one of the clauses of the federation, made America forever safe from enslavement.

---

ix. These covenants even constitute true violations rather than declarations of rights, since they assume that the living can engage the freedom of their descendants.

In 1776, Mr. Franklin became one of the representatives of the city of Philadelphia at the Pennsylvania convention, which chose him as president. The constitution of this state was in part his work. It differs from most of the others by a greater equality, and from all, in that the legislative power is entrusted to a single chamber of representatives;[18] Mr. Franklin's opinion alone determined this last provision. He thought that since enlightenment must naturally make rapid progress, especially in a country where revolution was going to provide new relations, the means to improve legislation should be made easy, and not surrounded with alien obstacles; and that, if the laws were so good as to make any change feared as harmful, the nation which had been enlightened enough to make them would no doubt also be enlightened enough not to destroy them.

He knew that a complicated constitution can be suitable for a people whom passing circumstances have driven toward freedom without their loving or knowing it; but that only a simple constitution is worthy of a people among whom love of liberty is the prime sentiment of all citizens, and the study of its principles the main employment of their reason. Mr. Franklin was aware that the procedure for debate in a single assembly can procure everything needed to give its decisions the deliberate maturity which guarantees their truth and wisdom; whereas the establishment of two chambers leads to avoiding new mistakes only by perpetuating existing errors. The contrary opinion is due to that discouraging philosophy which regards error and corruption as the normal state of societies, and moments of virtue and reason as wonders one cannot hope to make last. It was time for both a nobler and truer philosophy to preside over the destiny of humankind, and Mr. Franklin was worthy of setting the first example thereof.[x]

One forgives ancient legislations for having attempted to subject to eternal laws ignorant and crude men, who received as a gift from heaven these fruits of genius and virtuous enthusiasm, of which they could neither take in the scope, nor foresee the effects. But today, any legislator who would not address himself to reason alone would be an impostor, and he who

---

x. We will not hide the fact that, since Mr. Franklin's death, a new convention has divided the legislature of Pennsylvania into two chambers, either because the authority of example prevailed over reason, or because, having failed to take, in the first constitution, necessary precautions to prevent a single chamber from making decisions without serious discussion, without thoughtful reflection, and without being able to benefit from the help of enlightened public opinion, real difficulties were met and it was deemed preferable to resort to a remedy insufficient and dangerous, but already used, rather than try new ones.

would want to bind future generations to the inventions of his genius would be a tyrant.

No sooner had Pennsylvania's constitution been completed than Mr. Franklin was sent to negotiate with the Canadians. The Americans had attempted an attack on Quebec City and failed,[19] and these hostilities, by recalling the memory of an old animosity, could only make more difficult a reconciliation equally useful to both nations. The interests of the most influential citizens in Canada created further obstacles. The English had left the inhabitants with their own religion and laws. What was left of French nobility was afraid to join nations where the absolute prohibition of hereditary prerogatives was rightfully considered the aegis of liberty. The Roman Catholic clergy preferred being tolerated but protected by the English government, rather than to see freedom of opinion reign, which is always terrifying for men accustomed to ruling over minds. Mr. Franklin was not successful, and Canada remained faithful to the country where government offered the best hope of preserving a few abuses.

But it was in the Old World that Americans were to find support. Europe was favorably disposed towards them. The invention of printing had established rapid communication between nations where Latin was the common language of all educated men. They had ceased to be foreign to one another, and all men who could read had become fellow citizens. For a long time, religious quarrels were nearly the only fruit of this coming together; but when, through the progress of enlightenment, true science replaced systems, and a philosophy based on nature and observation supplanted the prejudices of the schools, enlightened men of all countries began to form only a single body, ruled by the same principles, and heading toward a single goal. Then, everywhere reason and freedom gained peaceful apostles, independent in their opinions, but united in their worship of these beneficent divinities. Soon, prejudice counted only ignorant or corrupt men among its followers, and talents or genius fought for the cause of truth alone. Each nation, according to its progress toward civilization, found itself subject more or less to the influence of two antagonistic parties, one benefitting alone from prejudices it was jealous to maintain, the other busy destroying them for the good of all. Sometimes, enlightenment would come down from the throne to reach the people; more often, it would rise up from the people to reach the throne, frightening in its wake those who, placed in between and benefitting from their ignorance and their mistakes, would have wanted to condemn them both to perpetual darkness. Thus, everywhere America could count on zealous and faithful friends, weak in each country, most often without apparent power, but strong in their noble agreement, and exercising a powerful influence over public opinion through the authority of reason and talents. Political circumstances further added to American hopes. France and Spain had not been able to forget the arrogance with which England had taken advantage of its latest victories. Gibraltar and the useless commissioner of Dunkirk,[20] which pride alone had maintained, were a permanent source of hatred.

For a long time Holland had seen with helpless distress the English sell their protection to the enemy of its freedom, so that the latter would make it easy for them to stunt Dutch trade. Believing themselves inaccessible on their island, and proud of that dominion over the sea which they thought eternal, they had become its tyrants, and there was no European power which they had neither hurt in its trade, nor offended by their arrogance. It was foreseeable that some would seize the opportunity to humble English power, and others would be satisfied with secretly applauding its losses. However, France, burdened with debt, ruled by weak ministers, held back by the memory of its latest defeats, had reason to fear seeing the peace needed for its recovery disturbed. Spain, which has in South America an empire larger, richer, and better situated than the English colonies, had reason to fear the contagious example of independence. The party favorable to England was still dominant in Holland, and the Americans had only made fruitless attempts there, and had obtained only uncertain and timid commitments, when Congress entrusted Mr. Franklin with negotiating with France.

At that time, he was the only man from America to enjoy a great reputation in Europe. Unable in their felicitous equality, and at the time of their political birth, to send an ambassador decorated in the eyes of prejudice with some of the trinkets of European vanity, or made illustrious by high offices, they chose a man who was great in the eyes of reason alone and famous because of his genius only. Their hopes were met with success. Mr. Franklin's fame in the sciences made all those who love or study them his friends, that is to say, all those who exercise a real and lasting influence on public opinion. When he arrived, he became an object of veneration for all enlightened men, and of curiosity for others. He would accept this curiosity with the natural easiness of his character, and the conviction that thereby he served the cause of his country. People considered it an honor to have seen him; they repeated what they had heard him say. Every house to which he consented to go, every festivity in his honor, would send out into society new admirers who also became supporters of the American Revolution.

He had understood ahead of time that he had to contend only with the indecision and weakness of ministers, that what he most needed to do was to bring the pressure of public opinion to bear upon them, to use fear to overcome their timidity; he knew that his mission was not really with them, but with the nation.

Men whom books of philosophy had secretly inclined to the love of liberty, became enthusiastic about the freedom of a foreign people, while waiting to be able to turn their attention to recovering theirs, and joyfully seized this opportunity to acknowledge sentiments publicly which prudence had forced them to keep silent.

No sooner had Mr. Franklin crossed the seas, than the genius of liberty had raised up that young hero who, born for freedom alone, was to devote his life to supporting it in America, to conquering it in France, and to serving it always, sometimes fighting on its behalf against the soldiers of tyranny, sometimes preventing vile enemies of the laws from sullying its triumph with acts of violence which their bloody hypocrisy dares to veil with its sacred name.[xi]

A general call soon arose in favor of war to support America, and the friends of peace did not even dare to complain that it was sacrificed to the cause of freedom. The ministers' willingness to accommodate the English aroused an indignation further increased by the out of place arrogance of their agents, and ten months after Mr. Franklin's arrival, the French ministry, carried along by public opinion, encouraged by the capture of an entire army forced to lay down its arms before American militias,[21] and concerned that English envoys had been sent to America with attractive proposals, finally signed a treaty of alliance with the United States.[22]

It has perhaps been criticized too much for being slow. France did not have a free constitution then; but French people were not slaves. While the people suffered under an arbitrary tyranny, and still more under the yoke of bad laws, souls were not enslaved, minds had retained their independence. It did not resemble those countries where there is only a despot, a treasury and an army; it was not immaterial whether war was consistent with or contrary to the wish of the nation, and the French already merited that their ministers follow the policy adopted among free nations, and that to declare war they wait for the voice of the people to call for it.

As a negotiator, Mr. Franklin would observe much and act little.

xi. M. de Lafayette.

He left it to the ministers of the allied powers to decide how to attack England and help America, afraid that an unfavorable outcome attributable to his advice or his requests would dampen their interest. He was particularly careful to foster in France the idea of American persistence and resourcefulness, and to maintain that enthusiasm which had been his work; while observing the movements of public opinion in England, he watched for the moment when the fall of the ministry that had wanted war would announce America's freedom. At last, he saw this moment come, and signed with a calm hand the safety and glory of his country, just as he had witnessed with steadfast resolution the dangers and setbacks it had faced. This calm did not reflect indifference, it resulted from a deep conviction that American independence could be purchased at a higher or a lower price, or recognized a few years later, but that it could not be at risk. It was the superiority of the mind of a man who knew that the moral world, like the physical world, is subject to fixed laws, and who foresaw in these immutable laws the triumph of his country. Above all, it reflected a very rare absence of any personal considerations; for it is their corrupting influence which so often tarnishes the love of freedom with those concerns, fears and furors which degrade it by making it too similar to the vile passions of interest and vanity. Mr. Franklin's patriotism had to be as calm as that of Socrates and Phocion, whom orators, who were bribed by factions or tyrants, also accused of not loving their country enough.

France, during this war, had presented him with scenes worthy of the interest of his observant genius. He had seen the same opinions censured when expressed in philosophical works, taken for granted in manifestoes; a people at peace in its ancient chains become intoxicated with the joy of breaking those borne in another hemisphere; republican principles openly advocated under an arbitrary government; the rights of men violated by the laws and by authority, but established and analyzed in books; political science worthy of the most enlightened century and the wisest people shine in the midst of countless absurd and barbaric institutions; the nation applauding the maxims of freedom at the theater, but obeying the maxims of servitude in its conduct: free in its sentiments and opinions, even in their expression, and appearing to see with indifference its actions remain subjected to laws it despised. It was easy for him to foresee that a people already so worthy of liberty was soon to recover it, and that the French Revolution, like the American, was one of those events which human reason can withdraw from the rule of chance and passions.

Mr. Franklin stayed in France after peace was signed, to try to tighten through trade the bonds created by gratitude and politics. European nations have invariably sacrificed in their laws the general interest of their citizens to that of wealthy speculators. But in America, the noble children of freedom had also liberated themselves from this shameful servitude, and had generously erected against the greedy schemes of the mercantilist spirit that shield against which the arrows of all tyrannies will forever break, their declaration of rights, all the more powerful because they understand its full implications, and because everyone, regarding it as the guarantee of his individual safety and tranquility, would be ashamed to sacrifice it to vile calculations of interest. The contrast between the commercial principles of Europe and America gave rise to difficulties that it was useful to remove; besides, it could be feared that habit, and similar tastes or customs, would enable England to keep an exclusive trade with America, and it was important to prevent this, because any exclusive trade, even if it is voluntary, always leads to a dangerous dependence.

Thus, Mr. Franklin seemed to wait peacefully in France for the end of his gentle and glorious life. Scholars, philosophers and friends of liberty were his fellow citizens, and serving his country was his consolation for the regret he felt in not enjoying the sight of its independence.

He led a more secluded, more peaceful life ever since his country had ceased needing to increase the number of its supporters. In his retreat in Passy, a small social circle, a few friends, and some easy work, filled the evening of a beautiful life. But a painful infirmity perturbed its course; from that moment on, his soul turned to his homeland, and he left France, to which, in exchange for its services, he left a great example and lessons which were not to remain useless for long. He set sail from a harbor in England, where he was accompanied by M. le Veillard who, during his stay in Passy, had faithfully looked after him with all the solicitude of filial affection, and had wished to postpone the painful moment of an eternal separation. But Mr. Franklin only touched the coast of England, and he generously spared his humbled enemies the sight of his glory. While he considered the French his friends, the English were for him relatives whose wrongs one likes to forget and in whom one must still respect the bonds of nature, even when their injustice has broken them.

His entry into Philadelphia was a triumph, and he had no need of a slave to let him know that he was only a mortal,[23] for nothing in this triumph belonged to chance.

All the bodies of government, all the citizens of the town, as well as the inhabitants of the countryside who had gathered together at the news of his ship's arrival, went to meet him; he walked along receiving the blessings of a free people, in whom an absence of several years had not weakened the gratitude for his services.

Soldiers who had spilled their blood for the independence secured by his courageous wisdom considered it an honor to show him their glorious wounds; he was surrounded by old men who had asked heaven to live long enough to see him once more, and by a new generation eager to get to know the features of the great man whose talents, services and virtues had aroused in their hearts the first outbursts of enthusiasm. He walked through this harbor now open to all nations; he saw once again, in a state of splendor, the public college and the hospital the founding of which had been one of his first acts of public service, the expansion of which was due to his wise foresight, and the success of which fulfilled his dearest wishes, the relief of human suffering and the progress of reason. He turned his eyes to this pleasant landscape, embellished by liberty, where, among the monuments of public prosperity, some remnants of English destruction only served to enhance the pleasures of peace and victory; and on that day, which recalled the sweet thoughts of his youth and the even sweeter memory of his useful labor, his soul gathered together in a single moment all the happiness and glory it had enjoyed in the course of a long life.

Soon afterwards he was elected president of Pennsylvania's assembly;[24] but he was destined to perform a last service for his country.

The American states had not yet set the makeup or authority of the congress which, entrusted with the common safety, was to make of thirteen independent republics a single power.

Mr. Franklin was one of the members of the convention which was to lay this last stone so necessary to the solidity of the noblest and most ambitious political edifice ever to be built by human reason. He was sorry to see that the majority wanted to give a complicated organization to an assembly which, by the nature of its functions, seemed to call for the simplest; to create useless counterweights to an authority which was almost never to be exercised over isolated and weak individuals, but only over powerful states; finally, to entrust a president, perhaps already too influential because of the length of his term, with a right of veto always dangerous to grant to a single man, and useless since such a power can be used neither to maintain unity in the laws, nor to produce activity in their execution. But it was a last tribute that America was unknowingly paying to the prejudices of the mother country. He was also sorry to see the same majority set the functions of Congress according to vague notions of utility and ideas belonging to ordinary politics, rather than on the basis of a thorough knowledge of the nature of societies and the rights of citizens. Nevertheless, the union between the thirteen states needed to be consolidated; and to dispose them all to accept the plan drawn up by the convention, he believed it necessary to provide the authority of the unanimous wish of their representatives.

Therefore, he signed; but, in a speech full of moderation and intelligence,[25] he let it be known that he had felt obliged to sacrifice his opinion to unanimity. This was tantamount to telling his fellow citizens: Accept this plan, the best proposal that the current state of opinion allows, and know how to postpone until another time the hope of a less-imperfect institution. Sacrifice to the need to acquire a political existence for the outside world this desire for perfection which, as long as the means to achieve it someday remain intact, could be a mistake resulting from pride rather than the fruit of an enlightened patriotism. His fellow citizens understood him, and America adopted this constitution, expressing wishes that future knowledge would erase the flaws that enlightened men thought it contained.

Mr. Franklin could not have refused the position of president of Pennsylvania's assembly without offending the feelings of gratitude and veneration which had called him to it despite his age and infirmities; but soon he gradually withdrew from public affairs to lead a life of honorable retirement, in touch with public life only through his wishes and memories. He had yielded to the entreaties of his friends who had asked him to write his memoirs, and this was the gentle occupation of his last years. He could look back upon the past without fear of regret or remorse; his life had been happy, pure[xii] and peaceful; thus, he would say *that he would willingly live it over again,* adding *that he would only wish to erase a few mistakes, like an author issuing a new edition of his work.*

His death was peaceful and accompanied only by that melancholy of a

---

xii. He had, during his long life, only one dangerous illness; it took him nearly to the grave; he contemplated death without fear, but not without needing some courage to renounce life, and it pained him to see that he would have to ready himself for death once more.

After his return to Philadelphia, his health gradually declined; for several years, he had been suffering from kidney stones, and he had wished to fight his illness with diet alone, because he thought this was enough to avert the worst pains, and because he did not want to purchase with a dangerous operation the uncertain hope of a few years of old age.

sensitive soul which, in leaving the objects it has loved, is disturbed neither by concern for their future, nor by painful memories of the past. He left to a beloved family a fortune acquired by his work and talents, the public gratitude attached to his name and the example of his life. He saw his country delivered from its ancient shackles, free to pursue happiness, and capable of finding it through reason, which he had himself freed from prejudices.

Humanity and candor formed the basis of his morals; a habitual cheerfulness, a gentle easiness in social life, and a quiet inflexibility in important matters made up his character. These last two qualities combine easily in men who, endowed with a superior mind and a strong soul, leave small things to doubt and indifference. His system of conduct was simple, he sought to use temperance and work to ward off grief and boredom: "Happiness," he would say, "like material bodies, consists of imperceptible elements." Without disdaining glory, he knew how to scorn the injustice of opinion, and, while enjoying gratitude, how to forgive envy.

In his youth, he had carried Pyrrhonism[26] to the very foundations of morals; the natural goodness of his heart and the soundness of his mind were his only guides, and they rarely led him astray. Later, he recognized that there was a moral science based on the nature of man, independent of all speculative opinions, preceding all conventions. He thought our souls received, in another life, the reward for their virtues and the punishment for their wrongs; he believed in the existence of a beneficent and just God to whom he paid, in the privacy of his conscience, a free and pure homage. He did not scorn public practices of religion, even thought they were useful to moral education, but he would seldom take part in them. All religions seemed to him equally good, as long as they followed the principle of universal tolerance and did not deprive of the rewards of virtue those who, while practicing it, embraced another creed, or did not profess any.

He left no single great work. His discoveries on electricity, which assure him everlasting fame, are contained in a few letters written to his friends. His other works on physics are also spread among letters; they always display ingenious and subtle views, more of that sagacity which analyzes objects and grasps their relationships, than of that mental power which combines and fathoms them.

Applying the physical sciences to everyday life, to domestic economy, was often the topic of his research; there, he found pleasure in proving that, even in the most common things, routine and ignorance are poor guides, and that we are very far from having exhausted what nature has in store in terms of resources for those who know how to study it.^{xiii}

On politics, he only wrote works prompted by circumstances. One can see that he always tries to reduce problems to their simplest elements, to explain them so that the least-educated men can understand and solve them. It is always to them that he addresses himself. Sometimes it is an error of which he wants to disabuse them, sometimes a useful truth for which he wants to gently prepare their minds, so that they accept it, and above all remember it. One would look in vain for a line he could be suspected of having written for his own glory.

He would often use those forms of writing which seem to conceal the truth only to make it more tangible, and, instead of teaching it, leave the pleasure of finding it out. Thus, while appearing to teach the surest means to reduce the size of a state deemed too difficult to govern, he brings to light the imprudent conduct of the English ministry with regard to America; or, to show the injustice of Great Britain's claims on its colonies, he imagines an edict by which the king of Prussia subjects England to taxation, under the pretext that the inhabitants of the banks of the Oder conquered or peopled it long ago.[27]

His conversation was like his style, always natural and often ingenious. In his youth, he had developed a taste for the Socratic method by reading Xenophon, and he enjoyed using it, sometimes asking shrewd questions to lead those who upheld a false opinion to refute it themselves; sometimes applying their own principles to familiar objects to force them to recognize the truth cleared of the clouds with which routine or prejudice had surrounded it; at other times, deciding by a fable, a tale or an anecdote, questions that the pedantry of a serious discussion would have obscured. Asked to request an end to the insulting practice of sending criminals to the colonies, a minister alleged to him the need to rid England of them. "What would you say," he replied, "if we ordered the exportation of rattlesnakes?"^{xiv}

Mr. Franklin had not elaborated a general system of politics for himself;

xiii. For a long time, and on several occasions, he worked on finding ways to improve chimneys, to combine fuel economy, heat intensity and evenness, and proper air circulation in heated places. Several years before he became famous, and at the time he began to enjoy financial independence, he was offered a patent for a stove he had invented; he refused. "I have benefitted from the inventions of others," he replied, "isn't it fair that they benefit from mine?"

xiv. I heard him tell this anecdote, which was ridiculously distorted in some of our newspapers.

he would examine problems as the course of events or his foresight would present them to his mind, and he would solve them with principles he drew from a pure soul and a sound and shrewd mind. In general, he seemed not to seek to give human institutions their highest degree of perfection immediately; he believed the most reliable course was to expect it over time; he was not obstinate in fighting openly against abuses, he found it more prudent to attack first the errors from which they sprang. In political as well as moral matters, he showed that sort of indulgence which is not excessively demanding because it is full of hope, and which forgives the present in favor of the future; he always proposed the measures most suited to maintaining peace, because it does not leave human happiness to chance, or hand over truth to partisan interests. He preferred the good obtained through reason to the one expected from enthusiasm, because it is more solid, more certain to come to pass, and lasts longer.

He feared as dangerous to the freedom and prosperity of society those exaggerated opinions behind which vain or superficial minds hide the inanity of their principles or the depravity of their projects. Above all, he detested that culpable Machiavellianism which is not ashamed to use, in the name of liberty, means condemned by justice, and which is not afraid to debase and endanger its cause by entrusting it to talents disgraced by vice. He who ventures to commit a crime to become free, he would say, would commit one without remorse to become master; and the man who has tarnished his life with treacherous or contemptible acts, incapable of loving freedom, only serves it to betray it.

In a word, his political philosophy was that of a man who believes in the power of reason and the reality of virtue, and who had wished to become the educator of his fellow citizens before being called to be their legislator.

His death was a day of mourning for friends of freedom in both worlds. No nation counted as a foreigner the man whose work, influence or example had been useful to all humankind. His fellow citizens remembered his fruitful efforts to accustom them to discussing their common affairs, and to spread among new generations the knowledge of their rights and duties; they compared what they were, when he first arrived in Philadelphia, to what they had become; they saw that his work to secure their independence was not his greatest gift, and that they owed him more than their freedom since it was thanks to him that they had become worthy of enjoying and retaining it. In England, he was mourned by all those who are not slaves of the ministry, or of prejudice.

The French National Assembly paid him a public tribute, and had the noble pride to acknowledge everything we owed to the American example and everything a nation can owe to the genius of a single man. By a fortunate circumstance, its president then was a philosopher who, like Franklin, had enlightened his fellow citizens about their rights before being chosen to restore them, and who, like him, regarded this honor only as a precious opportunity to carry out everything a strong soul and a superior mind had revealed to him for the happiness of men.[xv]

The Academy of Sciences had been eager to call into its midst the scientist who had snatched from nature one of its secrets and diverted one of its scourges; it greeted with enthusiasm the arrival of the philosopher who came to teach tyrants how to know justice, and men how to be subordinate only to their rights. It was pleased to see one of its members combine the glories of liberating both worlds, of enlightening America, and of setting the example of liberty for Europe. Always free in the midst of all tyrannies, the sciences convey to those who study them something of their noble independence; either they flee from countries subjected to arbitrary power, or they gently prepare the revolution which is to destroy it; they form a large class of men used to thinking for themselves, to taking pleasure in the search for truth and in the approbation of their peers, too enlightened, in the end, to fail to know their rights, even when they are prudent enough to wait silently for the moment to recover them. To the extent that their utility is independent of the revolutions of empires and the forms of government, that they do not abandon men to all the evils of ignorance when they experience those of servitude, and that they lighten and soften the chains of an enslaved people, they help to make the return to liberty faster, more peaceful and more certain. Let us compare the attempts of unenlightened centuries, so rarely crowned with lasting success and always sullied with wars, massacres and proscriptions, with the fruitful efforts of America and France; let us observe in the same century, but at different times, the two revolutions of fanatical and enlightened England,[28] we will see on one hand the contemporaries of Prynne and Knox who, while claiming to fight for heaven and freedom, cover their unfortunate country with blood to consolidate the tyranny of the hypocritical Cromwell; on the other, the contemporaries of Boyle and Newton establish with peaceful wisdom the freest constitution that could then exist on earth.

xv. The Abbé Sieyès.

Who can still fail to realize that nations do not have to choose between honoring the sciences and bending under the yoke of prejudice?[29] For, in the natural order of things, political enlightenment follows in their wake, relies on their progress, or can only cast, as among the ancients, an uncertain, passing and troubled light. Let us therefore be suspicious of those envious detractors who dare accuse them of thriving under despotism; undoubtedly, they are dimly aware that unenlightened nations are easier to deceive or control, that the more enlightened a people is, the more difficult it is to abuse popular support. They fear the patriotism of reason and virtue which hypocrisy can neither feign nor outwit; and, hiding the desire to rule behind the mask of enthusiasm for freedom, they seem to have recognized that, even under the freest constitution, an ignorant people is always enslaved.

APPENDIX

Notes to the French Translation of John Stevens's
Observations on Government (1789)

We translate here two of the long and numerous notes added by Condorcet, Pierre-Samuel Dupont de Nemours, and Jean-Antoine Gauvin-Gallois (and probably others; see our introduction, note 25) to the French translation of John Stevens's *Observations on Government* (1787, erroneously attributed to William Livingston), *Examen du gouvernement d'Angleterre, comparé aux constitutions des États-Unis* (Observations on the government of England compared to the constitutions of the United States), published by Froullé in 1789. The first (note 19, pp. 177–82, probably by Dupont de Nemours) sheds additional light on the views laid out by Condorcet in *Ideas on Despotism* on the topic of declarations of rights (above, sections 18–23). The second (note 28, pp. 225–40, perhaps by Condorcet and Mazzei) constitutes a new commentary on the Federal Constitution of 1787, which complements the one included in the supplement to Mazzei's *Researches on the United States* (see above).

Note 19

On What Must Be Understood by Legislative Authority, and to What Extent It Can Be Delegated

It is not enough to make it unlikely for the legislative power to be misused, it must be impossible.

Nations and even philosophers still have very vague ideas on *legislative authority*.

The authority to make any kind of law, even those that would be absurd and unjust, cannot be delegated to anyone, because it does not even belong to society as a whole.

If, prompted by fanatical ideas, society as a whole wanted to make a law contrary to the freedom, the safety, the right to property of the citizens, or of a single citizen, ordering, for example, that sorcerers be burned, as used to be done not so long ago throughout Europe, that firstborn sons be sacrificed or maimed, or exclusively children that are deformed or ugly (these barbaric laws have existed, some of them even in Sparta and in Rome), or just that part of the harvest be thrown into the river without compensating the owners; the isolated citizen who would oppose the enforcement of such a law could be oppressed by the greater strength of the others; he would probably wage an unsuccessful war against them, but he would not be *in rebellion*, and in overwhelming him with their power, the other citizens, society as a whole, would commit an act of tyranny.

We must therefore posit in principle that such *legislative authority*, understood in a broad sense, as would encompass the power to do or prohibit anything and everything, is a right that nature has reserved for itself, that no human association can appropriate, much less delegate.

Legislation in its entirety is contained in a good *declaration of rights*.

The nation assembled cannot grant anyone the authority to make laws contrary to the declaration of rights. In issuing this declaration, it has acknowledged what is just. No political body representing the nation can be corrupt enough to say openly: *I want the authority to do what is unjust*; no one will be foolish enough to grant anybody such authority.

What remains, therefore, is the *authority* to make *rules and regulations* the better to secure the preservation of rights: it is this *authority* which, in a limited sense, can be called *legislative*.

The word is perfectly suited to the thing, and would seem to suggest that at the origin of societies men had sounder principles and more accurate ideas than we ordinarily believe. They did not say LEGISFACTOR, which would have indicated the power to *make* laws arbitrarily; they said LEGISLATOR, *law bringer*, which implies that he who is entrusted with this respectable function has no other right than to take *the law* out of the immense store of nature, justice and reason, where it was *ready-made*, and bring it, raise it, present it to the people.

Ex natura, jus, ordo et leges. Ex homine, arbitrium, regimen et coercitio,[1] said the profound thinker Quesnay.[2]

Every *regulation* has a touchstone: *Is it in conformity with the declaration of rights, or not?*

Any citizen has the right to test it with this touchstone through a free discussion conveyed to the other citizens to the greatest extent possible. In this, the invention of printing is infinitely helpful;[3] this is why freedom of the press must be counted among the inalienable rights of each and every one.

However, this inalienable freedom to discuss *regulations*, which are improperly called *laws*, and compare them to the *declaration of rights*, which must include all the genuine laws of society, must never carry along with it the right to resist those whom society has put in charge of drafting and promulgating these rules. Public authority must always be guaranteed the provisional enforcement of its orders; and this itself is in keeping with the fundamental law or declaration of rights, which could not allow the arbitrary will or the opinion of a single individual, or several, to possibly undermine the general order of society.

But, the more it is necessary that the *regulation* or provisional order be strictly obeyed, the more important it is, if it is unjust, that this obedience not be prolonged beyond what is indispensable for good order, and that the declaration of rights may regain as soon as possible its full authority, and that the rule going against this declaration may be quickly amended.

Therefore, it is not at all a matter of indifference whether to delegate in whatever way the legislative authority belonging to man, or the authority to make regulations, for a year or for seven.

It cannot be delegated for less than a year, because nature, by giving us a harvest every year, has set for us a time to renew our political arrangements; it is the time when we can settle the expenses of government, and when the suspension of work in the fields grants us the leisure to confer together on greater objects.

There is, however, a rather serious drawback to always employing new and inexperienced men for the business of the state; and if one has served well, having served for some time is not a good reason to be dismissed from service.

To avoid this difficulty, without running into that of prolonging excessively the obedience due to provisional regulations which would be imperfect, the remedy is, it seems, to renew every year a considerable part of the council to which is entrusted the *authority* that is called *legislative*, leaving to the voters the power to elect the same individuals: so that a skilled and virtuous man could stay in office a long time, but only through a new election which secures this office for him for a short time only.

This measure, which should be applied to all public functions, has been adopted as far as legislative authority is concerned by all the United States of America, with the exception of Pennsylvania; and one can hope, based on the progress of their wisdom, that in the future they will take it as a rule in the renewal of all the representatives of their sovereignty.

Note 28

Observations on the Reflections of the Farmer from New Jersey Regarding the Project of Federal Constitution

The sound and profound reasoning of the farmer from New Jersey[4] regarding the fundamental flaws of the constitution of England and the illusion produced by the excessive use of vague or improper expressions, makes us regret that he did not pay as much attention to his reflections on the project of federal constitution. One may think, based on the date of his pamphlet, that the shortness of time was the main cause for this.

Every good American citizen, or better, every friend of humankind, will certainly wish to see demonstrated in fact "THAT MAN IS ACTUALLY CAPABLE OF GOVERNING HIMSELF, and not (through the imbecility of his nature) '*unavoidably*' necessitated to resign himself to the guidance of one or more masters."[5] No man with good sense and some knowledge could doubt this principle and would fail to recognize at the same time that, to put it into practice, our situation is much more favorable than ever has been that of any known people so far, ancient and modern; but he will not agree with the farmer from New Jersey that the best way to *teach mankind this important lesson* is to adopt the proposed constitution; he will not agree, unless several very essential changes are made to it.

"The man," he says, "who can deliberately go about to oppose the adoption of this plan, must evidently be actuated by sinister motives; for admitting it to be much more faulty than it really is, can we form any reasonable hope of obtaining a better?"[6] If such is really his opinion, how could he himself propose any changes?

No American ever so slightly judicious fails to understand the need for a good federal constitution. No one thinks that the proposed plan should be rejected entirely. Those who have compared its advantages and disadvantages express their opinion, or will do so, as is their right, as their duty requires, in short, as did the farmer from New Jersey. But it would be wrong to claim that a desire to see it improved, before it is adopted, is *evidence of sinister motives.*

The inactivity prevailing in the affairs of the union has more or less influence on the particular conduct of each state. For this reason, several citizens would like the constitution to be adopted as it is by enough states to set the matter in motion, in the hope that the difference of opinion of the minority, along with the positive effects of a free and general discussion, the desire to be united and the common interest in remaining so, would bring about the necessary changes.

Their intention is commendable, to be sure, and I do not believe this hope is ill founded. But can this justify insulting attacks against those who try to make its flaws known, along with all the evils to be expected from them? He who, out of selfishness, and because he would prefer an end to the current disorder over the happiness of future generations, would conceal them, could be accused with more justice. Certainly, if we had considered only the present generation, when we calculated, according to the probability of events, the amount of good and harm that we should expect, we would not have run the risk of a revolution. The same motive that prompted us originally, must still drive us today.

If the proposed constitution were unanimously accepted without making the necessary changes to it, and without even discussing its flaws, dire consequences for freedom could result. If bringing these flaws to light had been postponed until after its institution, there would have been reason to fear that ill-intentioned people would make the best citizens, the most zealous patriots, out to be enemies of public tranquility. The death of a few distinguished citizens, the people's predisposition in favor of the work of so many virtuous men, a natural inclination toward indolence, the delay in the appearance of the ill effects of a flawed institution, could have made the remedy impossible. Thus, whatever the resolution of the states may be, every American who takes an interest in the happiness of his descendants must insist on the necessity of a good federal constitution, and prove that the one which is currently being proposed cannot procure this benefit without several very essential changes.

The farmer from New Jersey admits that "the constitution, though excellent, is acknowledged on all hands to have its defects,"[7] but he also says, "When we consider the multiplicity of jarring interests, which mutual concession alone could reconcile, it really becomes matter of astonishment that a system of legislation could have been effected in which so few imperfections are to be found."[8]

The variety and opposition of interests are the only grounds upon which the supporters of the proposed constitution pretend to excuse its flaws. They could at most excuse those related to trade, as well as the complexity of the legislative body, by which each state enjoys its right in proportion to its population in one of the two chambers, whereas in the other chamber small states are on a par with large ones.[i] But how will the interest of even a single state ever require that in certain cases the president be granted more power than is compatible with good order and the preservation of freedom? That the same person be reeligible at each new election?[ii] That Congress itself set its own emoluments? That it render no account to the public except when it pleases, whereas the time when it would be required to do so should be laid down, and that it be given the right to organize elections in such a manner as to make it possible someday to establish a powerful oligarchy? Finally, it is hard to understand how a declaration of rights which would deprive of any pretext anyone who, in the future, would devise interpretations contrary to freedom, could be dangerous to any of the states.

Mr. Wilson, one of the deputies from Pennsylvania, a man of very distinguished talents, tries to demonstrate, in his apology of the proposed constitution, that a declaration of rights would be superfluous. He claims that in the constitution of a state, any power that the people does not explicitly reserve for itself is supposed granted to the representatives, and that on the contrary, in a federal constitution, everything which is not explicitly granted to the representatives is supposed reserved. He offers this assertion as an axiom, and consequently, does not assume that this could present any difficulty. According to his idea, there would not be a single declaration of rights issued by any of our states that is not absolutely useless because the maxims contained in all these declarations are indisputable and within the reach of everyone. It seems to me that Mr. Wilson would have reasoned more correctly if he had acknowledged the imperfection of the proposed

---

i. On this subject, one can read in the supplement to the *Historical and Political Researches* by the citizen of Virginia [i.e., Filippo Mazzei]: "Every complication in the system, every distinction is harmful by nature, and can only be justified by necessity. The other distinction between the Senate and the House of Representatives, pertaining to the influence of the various states, is a source of discord. . . .

"since resolutions of one of these bodies must be submitted for approval to the other, it is unlikely that such an expedient will produce the desired effect; if the smaller states believe themselves harmed by a resolution of the representatives, they will reject it in the Senate.

"It is a mistake to delude oneself into thinking that contrary principles can be reconciled. Such expedients will sometimes be useful, perhaps, as temporary remedies; they will never form the basis of a very solid structure" ["Supplement," 52–53 above].

ii. I will admit that the *reeligibility* of individuals is more in accordance with the true principles of liberty, and that it should not be prohibited, as long as it is certain that abuse of power cannot take place, and a larger majority is required to reelect the same person; but to reach certainty in this respect, it would be necessary to change the organization of government completely. The power that the proposed constitution grants the president is such that, rather than letting him be reeligible, I would consent to change him every other month like the doge of Lucca.

constitution in this respect, and had done justice to the writer who hastened to warn his fellow citizens about it and to demonstrate the necessity of a solemn declaration in which the power that the people could not, without imprudence, grant its agents, would be laid down as clearly as possible. Mr. Wilson's arguments on this point are such that every man who knows the superiority of his talents will draw from his very apology consequences unfavorable to his cause.

There has always been, and there is still, a dangerous error present among my fellow citizens. The bias in favor of the old constitution,[9] which has long been firmly entrenched, has in the end raised the notion of its alleged perfection to the status of an axiom; so that instead of regarding this false principle as the source of our current troubles, we have imagined them to come from the articles where we have deviated from it. The farmer from New Jersey was the first to fight against this error. He did not hesitate to point out flaws openly which afterwards he approves and accepts in the federal constitution, as if this constitution were not basically the same system: which only goes to prove that, although reason acts freely in theory, when putting principles into practice, it often finds itself smothered by prejudices.[iii]

"It is matter of surprise to me," this author says with regard to the parts which make up the English constitution, "that Messrs. Adams, De Lolme,[10] and others, should ever have thought of rearing a temple to liberty with such materials as these."[11] But in what way are the principles on which the constitution in question rests different? Surely the differences are not of a nature to reassure us. Neither the office of president, nor seats in the Senate, are hereditary. But that all these positions, and even those of representative, could very easily become so one day, will appear only all too likely to every attentive and unbiased mind.

He accepts the following principle, which cannot be disputed, "that no more power be delegated than is necessary to the due administration of government."[12] It does not take extraordinary attention to recognize that this *fundamental maxim*, without which a free government will never be able to maintain itself, has not been shown much respect.

"I did not intend," the citizen of Virginia says in the supplement to the *Historical and Political Researches on the United States*, "to examine scrupulously

---

iii. It is unbelievable that the farmer from New Jersey, who ridiculed so cleverly the system of balances, and so justifiably censured *this marshalling of power against power, in battle array* [*Observations on Government*, 29], noticed neither the imaginary balance, nor the contrast of powers that are included in the proposed constitution.

everything which would perhaps deserve a discussion; for example, whether the power granted to Congress is not such as to make the governments of the individual states almost powerless."[13] This topic deserves further discussion.

It is of the greatest importance that all the citizens of a free country be required, by the constitution itself, to attend to the administration of public affairs frequently and at fixed intervals. Being far from the place where public affairs are dealt with tends to dampen the zeal for public good, and too long an interval is liable to extinguish it. By contrast, a general and sustained attention fosters the spirit of equality, increases and spreads enlightenment, satisfies that sort of ambition which does credit to man and keeps, so to speak, the entire nation on the watch, so that seeds harmful to liberty can easily be smothered as soon as they appear.

Although the ancient proverb, *in avoiding Charybdis, he falls into Scylla,* is borne out every day, people derive little benefit from it. If the federal constitution does not have the necessary power, the citizens will always be ready to solve, for the common advantage, the problems which will possibly result from this flaw; but if its power is too great, a few individuals will inevitably be seen whose private interest will only seek to maintain, and even to increase it. They will form a closely united league; the body of the citizenry, scattered and divided, will not be able to put up any resistance, for lack of a central force. Experience teaches us only all too clearly that in such cases superiority in numbers is a weak resource.

The federal constitution once established, as it is proposed, and having gained strength, there is no business with which Congress could not meddle, and of which it could not deprive the governments of the individual states. This event would not happen immediately; ambitious men would prudently wait for the people to rest easy in the shade of security, and get accustomed to the new government. But as soon as the irresistible force of habit had begun to take root, fear and the love of tranquility would make it extremely easy to usurp the supreme power. The league would not be hard to form; fewer than one hundred individuals make up the House of Representatives, the Senate, the presidency and vice presidency. The troops and public treasury are at their disposal; they are judges of the numbers and amount needed, and have the right to levy men and money without being legally obliged either to disarm or give a financial account. One must not delude oneself into thinking that a domestic league can be discovered and dispersed as easily as a foreign league. Furthermore, it would be difficult to persuade minds to fight against it. For lack of legal means, one would be reduced to seeking one's only resource in an uprising, which even the most courageous men would perhaps oppose, held back by the horror of a civil war.[iv]

It is said that the president, if he wants to be renewed in his office, will be dependent upon public favor, and consequently that he will not fail to see to the people's interests, and oppose any design that could be pernicious. This reason is the most plausible of all to excuse the overly extensive power that the proposed constitution grants him. But then, could it not be asked whether it would not be better to avoid the problem rather than create it and make the remedy necessary? More importantly, this could not be a remedy, unless destiny, always favorable to America, supplies it with a succession of men equal in talents to General Washington. Otherwise, the people will only be left with nominating five individuals, from among whom the House of Representatives will elect the president, and the Senate the vice president. Let us see if this conjecture is well-founded.

In each state, the people must elect as many men as the state sends deputies to the two houses of Congress. Those elected must assemble and vote by ballot for two individuals, of whom at least one must be an inhabitant of a state different from their own. After the votes are counted, they must send the sealed report of the result to the president of the Senate, who must open it in the presence of the members of the two houses of Congress. If a single individual happens to have the votes of a majority of the electors of all the states, he is president, and the Senate must elect the vice president from among the five who have the most votes after him. If more than one person has a majority, the second is vice president. If no one happens to have a majority, the House of Representatives must elect the president from among the first five, and the Senate the vice president from among the four others and the first of the rest.[14]

It is easy to understand how unlikely it is that anyone would ever have a majority in an election of this nature, unless some citizen, because of extraordinary merit, acquires a universal reputation. But circumstances which enable great men to make a dazzling appearance are very rare. Besides, it is very likely that for us such circumstances will not present themselves anymore, and this is much to be desired. If several citizens of transcendent merit managed to make a great name for themselves, it would still be un-

---

iv. The term "civil war" has been wrongly applied to the Revolutionary War. Among the small number of Americans who refused to support the cause of freedom, very few fought against it; and if there happened to be Englishmen, relatives of Americans, who bore arms in these circumstances, their number must have been very insignificant, since no information has been reported about them.

likely that any of them would have a majority, and the unlikelihood would be in proportion to their number. If there were four, and they were first on the list, the representatives could exclude them all, and prefer the fifth, although without merit, if they found him more amenable to their views.

In any case, since the new constitution explicitly states that to make necessary changes to it the combined votes of nine states will be enough,[15] its adoption is desirable despite all its flaws. Remedy will be possible when only the support of nine states is needed. According to the current constitution, the support of all thirteen states is necessary; and reason, experience, in short, everything, demonstrates the absurdity of such a law. Nothing could be more absurd than to require the perfect unanimity of thirteen states whenever something to amend is found in their federal constitution. One might as well, as it were, forbid ever making any changes to it.

This would amount to the *liberum veto* of the Poles.[16] All your troubles, someone told Dutch patriots not long ago, come from this error of your *so-called* constitution which, in several important cases, requires a perfect unanimity. If your ancestors had looked up the definition of *perfect unanimity* in the dictionary of common sense, they would have found *permanent discord*. "Unanimity," Count Wielhorski said, "goes against the spirit and purpose of all societies; very far from contributing to the preservation of freedom, it only works towards destroying equality among citizens; he who uses the right of liberum veto, natural consequence of unanimity, binds the will of all his fellow citizens, and acts with them in the most despotic way."[v]

The unanimity required by the current constitution of the United States can only be extremely rare. The most useful improvements will be proposed in vain; a single state that does not see fit to accept them will be enough, and the alliance of the twelve others will be forced to yield to the interest or whim of only one. Thus, evil takes root, spreads, multiplies, and can only be destroyed by the most violent remedies.[vi]

v. *Essai sur le rétablissement de l'ancienne forme du gouvernement de Pologne* [Essay on the restoration of the ancient form of the government of Poland], London, 1775, pages 168–69 [my translation].

vi. The reader who would like more details on the new constitution can consult the supplement to the *Historical and Political Researches on the United States*.

1743   September 17: Birth of Marie-Jean-Antoine-Nicolas Caritat, marquis de Condorcet, in Ribemont, Picardy. The Caritats de Condorcet, Protestants who had converted back to Catholicism, were an old noble family from the Dauphiné. Condorcet's father, captain of a regiment of cavalry, is killed during training maneuvers five weeks after the birth of his son. The child is brought up by his mother, a very religious woman of bourgeois origin, who is entirely devoted to her only son.

1754–58   Studies with the Jesuits in Reims.

1758–59   Studies at the Collège de Navarre in Paris. September 1759: At sixteen, Condorcet defends a thesis on calculus, which captures d'Alembert's interest.

1762   Condorcet settles in Paris, rue Jacob, to devote himself to the study of mathematics.

1763   Condorcet meets Lagrange, the great mathematician. End of the Seven Years' War. France loses almost all of its colonies in North America. England, deeply in debt because of the war, seeks to impose new taxes on its colonies.

1765   *Du calcul intégral* (On integral calculus). D'Alembert, who has taken Condorcet under his wing, introduces his protégé into the salon of Mlle de Lespinasse, where he gets to know the philosophes and encyclopedists.

1767   *Du problème des trois corps* (On the three-body problem).

1768   *Essais d'analyse* (Essays on calculus).

1769   At twenty-five, Condorcet is admitted to the Royal Academy of Sciences. He and Turgot become friends.

1770   September–October: Condorcet and d'Alembert spend two weeks with Voltaire at Ferney.

1772   Franklin is elected to the Academy of Sciences.

1774   May: Death of Louis XV. August: Turgot becomes head of the government and tries, without success, to introduce sweeping economic, financial, administrative, and political reforms in the kingdom.

1775   January: Condorcet is appointed *inspecteur général des monnaies*. He will hold the office until 1790. He is elected to the American Philosophical Society, founded by Franklin. Beginning of the American Revolutionary War. *Lettres sur le commerce des grains* (Letters on the grain trade).

1776   Condorcet becomes permanent secretary of the Academy of Sciences. May: Fall of Turgot. Condorcet wants to resign from his position as inspecteur des monnaies, but his resignation is refused. June 12: Adoption of the first American declaration of rights, that of Virginia. July 4: Declaration of Independence. September 28: Ratification of the first constitution of Pennsylvania. December: Franklin arrives in Paris as American commissioner to France. Officially appointed ambassador in 1778, he will remain in France until 1785.

1777   Drafting of the first constitution of the United States, the Articles of Confederation (ratified in 1781). American victory at the Battle of Saratoga.

1778   Treaty of Alliance between France and the United States.

1780   *Observations de Condorcet sur le 29e livre de "l'Esprit des lois"* (Observations by Condorcet on the twenty-ninth book of *The Spirit of the Laws*).

1781   *Réflexions sur l'esclavage des nègres* (Reflections on negro slavery). Decisive Franco-American victory at the Battle of Yorktown.

1781–84 Condorcet's scientific work focuses mainly on the theory of probability and its applications to the study of social phenomena.

1782   *Discours de réception à l'Académie Française* (*Reception Speech at the French Academy*).

1783   Treaty of Paris, which puts an end to the Revolutionary War.

1784   Jefferson arrives in Paris.

1785   *Essai sur l'application de l'analyse à la probabilité des décisions rendues à la pluralité des voix* (Essay on the application of calculus and probability theory to collective decision-making). Jefferson succeeds Franklin as American ambassador to France, a position he will hold until September 1789. Condorcet becomes an honorary freeman of the city of New Haven, Connecticut. *Vie de Voltaire* (Life of Voltaire); *Œuvres complètes de Voltaire* (*Complete Works of Voltaire,* 1785–89), edited by Beaumarchais, Condorcet, and Decroix (Kehl edition).

1786 *Influence de la Révolution de l'Amérique sur l'Europe* (*Influence of the American Revolution on Europe*). Condorcet marries Marie-Louise-Sophie de Grouchy, twenty-one years his junior. Their marriage will be a happy one, despite their age difference, due to the common interests that unite the couple. A brilliant young woman, Sophie de Condorcet will host a prominent salon at the Hôtel des Monnaies, quai de Conti. Among her guests were Lafayette, Jefferson, Thomas Paine, Malesherbes, Mirabeau, Beccaria, Adam Smith, Destutt de Tracy, Cabanis, Garat, Volney, Marmontel, Grimm, the Abbé Morellet, Beaumarchais, Suard, La Harpe, Chamfort, Chénier, Olympe de Gouges, Mme de Staël, and Benjamin Constant. Shays' Rebellion in Massachusetts (1786–87). *Vie de Monsieur Turgot* (Life of Monsieur Turgot).

1787 Convention in Philadelphia and drafting of a new constitution of the United States (ratified in 1788).

1788 Condorcet publishes a commentary on the new American constitution in the supplement to Filippo Mazzei's *Recherches historiques et politiques sur les États-Unis de l'Amérique Septentrionale* (Historical and political researches on the United States of North America), a work that already included two of his essays: a second edition of *Influence de la Révolution de l'Amérique sur l'Europe*, and *Lettres d'un bourgeois de New Haven à un citoyen de Virginie, sur l'inutilité de partager le pouvoir législatif entre plusieurs corps* (*Letters from a Freeman of New Haven to a Citizen of Virginia on the Futility of Dividing the Legislative Power Among Several Bodies*). He joins the Société des amis des noirs (Society of the friends of black people), an abolitionist club founded by Brissot at the beginning of the year. He will become its president the following year. *Essai sur la constitution et les fonctions des assemblées provinciales* (*Essay on the Constitution and Functions of the Provincial Assemblies*); *Lettres d'un citoyen des États-Unis, à un Français, sur les affaires présentes* (Letters from a citizen of the United States to a Frenchman on current affairs).

1789 March–May: Condorcet prepares the *Cahier de doléances* of the nobility of Mantes but does not succeed in getting himself elected to represent it at the Estates General. He also contributes to the drafting of the cahier of the nobility of Paris but again fails to get elected: neither the nobility nor the third estate selects him.

Therefore, he will not be a member of the National Assembly (Assemblée nationale constituante). September: Condorcet is elected to the municipal assembly of Paris. December: Condorcet is elected president of the committee charged with drafting a new municipal plan for Paris. *Idées sur le despotisme* (*Ideas on Despotism*); *Sur la forme des élections* (*On the Form of Elections*); Condorcet contributes to the notes appended to the French translation of a pamphlet by John Stevens, *Observations on Government* (1787) (*Examen du gouvernement d'Angleterre, comparé aux constitutions des États-Unis*).

1790   Spring: Condorcet founds, with Sieyès, the Société de 1789, a club of moderate reformers active until the beginning of 1791, and edits, with Dupont de Nemours, the *Journal de la Société de 1789*, which is issued between June and September and where he publishes *Sur l'admission des femmes au droit de cité* (*On the Admission of Women to the Rights of Citizenship*). April 17: Death of Franklin. August: Condorcet loses his seat in the assembly of the Commune of Paris. November: *Éloge de M. Franklin* (*Eulogy of Franklin*). Adoption of a new bicameral constitution by Pennsylvania. Birth of Condorcet's daughter, Éliza.

1791   *Cinq mémoires sur l'instruction publique* (Five memoirs on public instruction), which appear in the *Bibliothèque de l'homme public* (1790–92) (Library of the public man), a periodical co-edited by Condorcet. April: On Mirabeau's recommendation, the king appoints Condorcet one of the six administrators of the treasury. After the king's flight in June, Condorcet becomes republican and resigns from his position at the treasury. July: Champ de Mars massacre. Break with Lafayette. September: Condorcet is elected to the Legislative Assembly. October: Condorcet is elected president of the committee on public instruction of the Legislative Assembly. Ratification of the U.S. Bill of Rights.

1792   February: Condorcet is elected president of the Legislative Assembly. July: Condorcet becomes president of the Commission of Twenty-One of the Legislative Assembly, a veritable executive power. August: Fall of the monarchy. September: Condorcet is elected to the National Convention. October: Condorcet is elected to the constitution committee of the Convention. He will play a leading role in it, acting as its rapporteur. December: Trial of the king.

1793   January 21: Execution of Louis XVI. Condorcet had voted to convict the king but against the death penalty. February: Condorcet presents the Girondin constitution, of which he is the main author, to the Convention, *Plan de constitution, présenté à la Convention nationale les 15 et 16 février 1793* (Constitutional plan presented to the National Convention, on February 15 and 16, 1793). May: The Girondin constitution is set aside by the Convention without being voted on. June 2: The Convention orders the arrest of the Girondins. Condorcet, who is close to the Girondins but has remained independent, is spared for the moment. June 24: Hasty imposition of a Jacobin constitution that will, in fact, never be applied. Condorcet protests in *Aux citoyens français, sur la nouvelle constitution* (To the citizens of France, on the new constitution). June–July: Publication of the *Journal d'instruction sociale*, edited by Condorcet and Sieyès, in which appears the *Tableau général de la science qui a pour objet l'application du calcul aux sciences politiques et morales* (General Survey of the Science Concerning the Application of Calculus to the Political and Moral Sciences). July 8: The Convention orders Condorcet's arrest. He takes refuge rue des Fossoyeurs (today rue Servandoni), near the Luxembourg Gardens, at the home of a widow who rents rooms, Mme Vernet. July 28: Decree by the Convention declaring the Girondins traitors to the homeland (*traîtres à la patrie*). Although spared by this decree, Condorcet issues a vigorous protest in a *Lettre à la Convention nationale* (Letter to the National Convention). September: Beginning of the Terror. October 3: Condorcet is included in the decree of accusation against the Girondins voted by the Convention. October 31: Execution of the Girondins. In hiding, Condorcet writes the *Esquisse d'un tableau historique des progrès de l'esprit humain* (Outline of a historical chart of the progress of the human mind). *Fragment sur l'Atlantide, ou efforts combinés de l'espèce humaine pour le progrès des sciences* (Fragment on the New Atlantis; or, Combined Efforts of the Human Species for the Advancement of Science); *Lettre de Junius à William Pitt* (Letter from Junius to William Pitt); *Sur les élections* (On Elections).

1794   March 25: Fearing that his refuge has been discovered, Con-
        dorcet leaves the rue des Fossoyeurs and travels on foot to the
        village of Fontenay-aux-Roses (now a southern suburb of Paris)
        to seek help from his former friends the Suards, who own a house
        there. The Suards are not home and Condorcet wanders in the
        surrounding countryside for nearly two days. March 27: Early in
        the morning, Condorcet finally finds the Suards at home but
        they turn him away. He is arrested early in the afternoon at an
        inn, in nearby Clamart, and then taken to jail in Bourg-la-Reine.
        March 29: Condorcet is found dead in his cell. It is not clear
        whether he committed suicide or, more probably, succumbed to
        exhaustion. July 27 (9 Thermidor, Year II): Fall of Robespierre.

1795   Posthumous publication of the *Esquisse d'un tableau historique des
        progrès de l'esprit humain*. The Convention orders the purchase and
        distribution in the schools of three thousand copies of the *Esquisse*.

NOTES

INTRODUCTION

1. Besides Condorcet, the leading américanistes on the eve of the French Revolution were Lafayette, of course, Brissot de Warville, Dupont de Nemours, the duc de La Rochefoucauld d'Enville, Crèvecœur, and the marquis de Chastellux.

2. The *History of the East and West Indies* was not the work of Raynal alone but of several contributors, chief among them Diderot. In the "definitive" 1780 edition, chapters 1–5 and 18–30 of book 17, and 1–37 of book 18 deal with colonial America; chapters 38–52 of book 18 cover the Revolution. See the 1783 English translation, Guillaume-Thomas Raynal, *A Philosophical and Political History of the Settlements and Trade of the Europeans in the East and West Indies*, trans. John O. Justamond, 8 vols. (London: W. Strahan & T. Cadell, 1783). The chapters on the Revolution are also available as Raynal, *The Revolution of America* (1783; Boston: Gregg Press, 1972). Selections from the chapters on colonial America can be found in Raynal, *A History of the Two Indies*, trans. and ed. Peter Jimack (Aldershot, U.K.: Ashgate, 2006), 242–61.

3. Filippo Mazzei, *Recherches historiques et politiques sur les États-Unis de l'Amérique Septentrionale*, 4 vols. (Colle, Va., and Paris: Chez Froullé, 1788). This early history of the United States devotes two of its four volumes to refuting the reservations expressed by Raynal and Mably concerning the future of the new republic. Inserted in the other two volumes are two essays by Condorcet: a second edition of *Influence de la Révolution de l'Amérique sur l'Europe* (1786) (4:237–83) [*Influence of the American Revolution on Europe*], and *Lettres d'un bourgeois de New Haven à un citoyen de Virginie, sur l'inutilité de partager le pouvoir législatif entre plusieurs corps* (1:267–371) [*Letters from a Freeman of New Haven to a Citizen of Virginia on the Futility of Dividing the Legislative Power Among Several Bodies*], an important theoretical text on social choice, which we do not include in the present volume, however, since it is not specifically about the United States. A translation of Mazzei's work is available, but it omits the two essays by Condorcet. See Philip Mazzei, *Researches on the United States*, trans. and ed. Constance D. Sherman (Charlottesville: University Press of Virginia, 1976).

4. See Durand Echeverria, *Mirage in the West: A History of the French Image of American Society to 1815* (New York: Octagon Books, 1966 [1957]), 71, 162.

5. Condorcet also knew John Adams, but the two men disagreed sharply on political matters.

6. For more on the Girondin constitution, which was never voted on, see *On the Principles of the Constitutional Plan Presented to the National Convention* [*Plan de constitution, présenté à la Convention nationale les 15 et 16 février 1793: Exposition des principes et des motifs du plan de constitution*], in Condorcet, *Selected Writings*, ed. Keith M. Baker (Indianapolis: Bobbs-Merrill, 1976), 143–82 (also translated as *A Survey of the Principles Underlying the Draft Constitution*, in *Condorcet: Foundations of Social Choice and Political Theory*, trans. and ed. Iain McLean and Fiona Hewitt [Aldershot, U.K.: Edward Elgar, 1994], 190–227); and David Williams, *Condorcet and Modernity* (Cambridge: Cambridge University Press, 2004), 266–76; Victor G. Rosenblum, "Condorcet as Constitutional Draftsman," in *Condorcet Studies I*, ed. Leonora C. Rosenfield (Atlantic Highlands, N.J.: Humanities Press, 1984), 187–205; Keith M. Baker, *Condorcet: From Natural Philosophy to Social Mathematics* (Chicago: University of Chicago Press, 1975), 320–30. On the posthumous influence of Condorcet and the Girondin constitution,

see Keith M. Baker, "Condorcet," in *A Critical Dictionary of the French Revolution*, ed. François Furet and Mona Ozouf, trans. Arthur Goldhammer (Cambridge: Harvard University Press, 1989), 209–12.

7. The reception of Condorcet's works in the nineteenth century (and beyond) is a complex topic. The radical, republican ideas of the philosopher and revolutionary often made him a controversial figure.

His project for a rational social science remained a central reference for the *idéologues* during the Directory and the Empire. Later, Saint-Simon and Comte claimed to prolong and develop his philosophy of progress, but they inflected it in a direction foreign to Condorcet's thought. Laplace and Poisson, the great late eighteenth- and early nineteenth-century mathematicians, built on his research on elections, but his theory of voting was soon after forgotten, not to be fully rediscovered until the second half of the twentieth century. Only his reflections on public instruction remained influential throughout the nineteenth century.

Among the political texts, the writings on the United States seem to have quickly fallen into oblivion. Constant, who started regularly attending Mme de Condorcet's salon before the Revolution, and who, of all the great liberal thinkers of the nineteenth century, was closest to Condorcet, acknowledged his debt to the philosophe in his famous analyses of the differences between "ancient" and "modern" liberty. See Benjamin Constant, *The Spirit of Conquest and Usurpation and Their Relation to European Civilization* (1814) [*De l'esprit de conquête et de l'usurpation, dans leurs rapports avec la civilisation européenne*], 103n2 (pt. 2, chap. 6), and "The Liberty of the Ancients Compared with That of the Moderns" (1819) ["De la liberté des anciens comparée à celle des modernes"], 312, both in *Political Writings*, trans. and ed. Biancamaria Fontana (Cambridge: Cambridge University Press, 1988). But he makes no mention, in his political works, of Condorcet's writings on the United States. As for Tocqueville, he never alludes to Condorcet in *De la démocratie en Amérique* (1835/40) [*Democracy in America*]. This silence is not too surprising considering his generally critical attitude toward the philosophes. See *L'Ancien Régime et la Révolution* (1856) [*The Old Regime and the Revolution*], bk. 3, chap. 1.

8. Donald S. Lutz has established the preeminence of Montesquieu as the authority of reference in American revolutionary literature. See "The Relative Influence of European Writers on Late Eighteenth-Century American Political Thought," *American Political Science Review* 78, no. 1 (1984): 189–97.

9. See Bernard Manin, "Montesquieu," in Furet and Ozouf, *Dictionary of the French Revolution*, 728–41; Joyce Appleby, "America as a Model for the Radical French Reformers of 1789," *William and Mary Quarterly* 28, no. 2 (1971): 267–86. The defeat of the *Monarchiens*, proponents of an English-style constitution, came on September 10 and 11, 1789, when the National Assembly voted to reject a bicameral legislature and an unlimited royal veto.

10. Constant, "The Liberty of the Ancients Compared with That of the Moderns," in *Political Writings*, 309–28.

11. See Keith M. Baker's "Political Languages of the French Revolution," in *The Cambridge History of Eighteenth-Century Political Thought*, ed. Mark Goldie and Robert Wokler (Cambridge: Cambridge University Press, 2006), 626–59; "Defining the Public Sphere in Eighteenth-Century France: Variations on a Theme by Habermas," in *Habermas and the Public Sphere*, ed. Craig Calhoun (Cambridge, Mass.: MIT Press, 1992), 181–211; and "Condorcet," in Furet and Ozouf, *Dictionary of the French Revolution*, 204–12.

12. By contrast, Montesquieu's concept of *esprit général* (general spirit) (see *The Spirit of the Laws*, bk. 19) and Diderot's very Montesquieuan ideas on the role of *opinion publique* (as expressed, for instance, in chaps. 35 and 39 of bk. 18 of the *History of the East and West Indies*, on America) allow for a much greater measure of influence from national tradition. See my own essay, "Variations on Montesquieu: Raynal and Diderot's *Histoire des deux Indes* and the American Revolution," *Journal of the History of Ideas* 70, no. 3 (2009): 399–420, esp. 407–8.

13. *Influence of the American Revolution on Europe*, "Introduction."

14. Ibid., 23.

15. Condorcet, *Lettres d'un citoyen des États-Unis, à un Français, sur les affaires présentes* (1788) [Letters from a citizen of the United States to a Frenchman on current affairs], in *Œuvres de Condorcet*, ed. A. Condorcet O'Connor and M. F. Arago, 12 vols. (Paris: Firmin Didot, 1847), 9:102 (my translation). This is another text that, despite its title, is not specifically about the United States; it deals chiefly with the political situation in France in 1788.

16. *American Revolution*, 23. See also *Ideas on Despotism* (1789) [*Idées sur le despotism*], sec. 17.

17. Baker, *Condorcet*, 212.

18. *American Revolution*, 24.

19. *The Spirit of the Laws*, bk. 5, chaps. 3–7.

20. *Letters from New Haven* (1787), in McLean and Hewitt, *Condorcet*, 333.

21. Tocqueville later singled out equality of social conditions as the essence of democracy as a social phenomenon. See the very beginning of *Democracy in America*, trans. Gerald E. Bevan (London: Penguin, 2003), 11.

22. Montesquieu himself, when defining honor as the principle of monarchy and the privilege of a hereditary nobility, had specified that, philosophically speaking, this honor is a false one (*The Spirit of the Laws*, bk. 3, chap. 7). Nevertheless, Condorcet cannot refrain from a critical reference to *The Spirit of the Laws*: "We [Europeans] said, not so long ago, that the sense of honor can fully exist only in certain social classes and that it was necessary to degrade the greater part of a nation in order to give the rest a little more pride." *American Revolution*, 30.

23. *American Revolution*, 34–35. Franklin, of course, provided Condorcet with a perfect illustration of what this new human type, the enlightened American, might be like.

24. Ibid., 25.

25. Sections 18–23. The same insistence on the necessity of a declaration of rights can also be found in the long notes appended to the French translation of John Stevens's pamphlet, erroneously attributed to William Livingston, *Observations on Government* (1787): *Examen du gouvernement d'Angleterre, comparé aux constitutions des États-Unis* [Observations on the government of England compared to the constitutions of the United States] (London and Paris: Chez Froullé, 1789). See the appendix. The anonymous notes to this translation are usually attributed to Condorcet, Pierre-Samuel Dupont de Nemours, and Jean-Antoine Gauvin-Gallois. However, the editors' foreword, which indicates that "some American, Italian and French writers have contributed to this work" (vii, my translation), implies that others were also involved, most likely Mazzei and perhaps Jefferson and Paine. Notes 19 and 28, the most relevant for this volume, are not among the ones that are known for certain to have been drafted by Condorcet. Note 19 is probably by Dupont de Nemours. As for note 28, the continuity between the supplement to Mazzei's *Researches on the United States* and this note leads us to believe that the latter text, like the former, was authored by Condorcet and Mazzei. In any case, and as the editors' foreword itself suggests ("One will recognize [in this work] different pens, but very similar principles" [vii, my translation]), one can legitimately regard the notes to *Examen du gouvernement d'Angleterre* as a collective work reflecting opinions shared by all the anonymous authors.

26. *American Revolution*, 26.

27. *The Spirit of the Laws*, bks. 14–17.

28. Ibid., bk. 11.

29. *American Revolution*, 29. Montesquieu had famously said, "So that one cannot abuse power, power must check power by the arrangement of things." *The Spirit of the Laws*, trans. and ed. A. M. Cohler, B. C. Miller, and H. S. Stone (Cambridge: Cambridge University Press, 1989), 155 (bk. 11, chap. 4).

30. *American Revolution*, 35. Hence the crucial role of public education in Condorcet's political theory. It provides the all-important link between public opinion and the general will on one hand, and the rationality of the law on the other.

31. The principal exponent of this influential theory in the second half of the eighteenth century was the Dutch philosopher Cornelius de Pauw in his *Recherches philosophiques sur les Américains* (1768) [Philosophical researches on the Americans]. Inspired by Montesquieu's theory of climate and above all by Buffon, who had claimed that the flora and fauna of the New World were underdeveloped compared to those of the Old, de Pauw expanded the thesis to include human populations, both native and transplanted from Europe. The American climate is so inhospitable to life, so the theory goes, that humans living in the New World soon show signs of physical as well as mental degeneration. The classic book on this topic is Antonello Gerbi's *The Dispute of the New World: The History of a Polemic, 1750–1900*, trans. Jeremy Moyle (Pittsburgh: University of Pittsburgh Press, 1973), 3–288, on the Enlightenment.

32. Condorcet was a staunch advocate of free trade and opposed all taxes on commerce, on the grounds that they were counterproductive economically and constituted infringements on the natural rights of freedom and property.

33. Constant, *The Spirit of Conquest and Usurpation*, 52–55 (pt. 1, chap. 2).

34. See Horst Dippel, "Condorcet et la discussion des constitutions américaines en France avant 1789," in *Condorcet, homme des Lumières et de la Révolution*, ed. Anne-Marie Chouillet and Pierre Crépel (Fontenay/Saint-Cloud, France: ENS Éditions, 1997), 204.

35. Under the Articles of Confederation, Congress consisted of a single chamber, in which each state's delegation had one vote. This single house combined legislative and executive functions: it appointed a president (the president of Congress), a committee of the States to serve when Congress was not in session (with one member from each state), and other committees or officers. However, Congress and the central government had very limited jurisdiction; most powers remained with the states.

36. "Supplement," 52.

37. On Condorcet's opposition to bicameralism, see *Letters from New Haven*, letter 4, 325–33, as well as "Condorcet and the Americans: Bicameralism and the Separation of Powers," in McLean and Hewitt, *Condorcet*, 64–69; and Max M. Mintz, "Condorcet's Reconsideration of America as a Model for Europe," *Journal of the Early Republic* 11, no. 4 (1991): 493–506.

38. "Supplement," 53.

39. See also in the appendix, *Examen du gouvernement d'Angleterre*, 114.

40. Ibid., 116.

41. See *Ideas on Despotism*, sec. 21.

42. See *Eulogy of Franklin* (1790) [*Éloge de M. Franklin*, 1790], 95.

43. See *Principles of the Constitutional Plan*, 155–65.

44. See *Letters from New Haven*, letters 2 and 3, 295–324; and *Principles of the Constitutional Plan*, 146–55.

45. *American Revolution*, 41.

46. Ibid., 26.

47. *Examen du gouvernement d'Angleterre*, note 22, 200–201 (my translation). This note is probably by Dupont de Nemours.

48. Franklin was very popular in France, where he had skillfully exploited, for the benefit of his diplomatic mission, the positive stereotypes depicting Americans as an enlightened, freedom-loving people, and, at the same time, as a people whose manners and spirit reflected the simplicity of nature. In addition to Condorcet's, the most important eulogies of Franklin were those delivered by Mirabeau at the National Assembly on June 11, 1790, by the duc de La Rochefoucauld before the Société de 1789 on June 13, by the Abbé Fauchet on behalf of the Commune of Paris on July 21, and by Vicq d'Azyr, secretary of the Royal Society of

Medicine, on March 14, 1791. Condorcet's *Eulogy* stands out from these other speeches by its more pronounced character as a philosophical manifesto. See Alfred O. Aldridge, *Franklin and His French Contemporaries* (New York: New York University Press, 1957), 212–34.

49. See Jürgen Habermas, *The Structural Transformation of the Public Sphere: An Inquiry into a Category of Bourgeois Society*, trans. Thomas Burger with Frederick Lawrence (Cambridge, Mass.: MIT Press, 1989).

50. *Eulogy of Franklin*, 82.

51. Ibid., 88, 86, 103, 106.

52. Ibid., 103, 104–5.

53. Ibid., 85, 84, 88–89.

54. Ibid., 95.

55. Ibid., 94, 90–91. "The great advantage enjoyed by Americans is to have reached democracy without the sufferings of a democratic revolution and to have been born equal instead of becoming so" (*Democracy in America*, 591 [vol. 2, part 2, chap. 3]), wrote Tocqueville, who developed this idea of continuity to make it a central theme of *Democracy in America*. See notably vol. 1, part 1, chap. 2.

56. *Eulogy of Franklin*, 96.

57. "In meditating on the nature of the moral sciences, one cannot indeed help seeing that, based like the physical sciences upon the observation of facts, they must follow the same methods, acquire an equally exact and precise language, attain the same degree of certainty." *Reception Speech at the French Academy* (1782) [*Discours de réception à l'Académie Française*], in *Selected Writings*, 6. See also the beginning of the introduction to *Essay on the Application of Mathematics to the Theory of Decision-Making* (1785) [*Essai sur l'application de l'analyse à la probabilité des décisions rendues à la pluralité des voix*], in *Selected Writings*, 33.

58. *Eulogy of Franklin*, 99, 107, 106. And just as the spirit of scientific inquiry inevitably gives rise to the spirit of liberty, likewise only a free constitution can truly foster progress in the sciences. See the excerpt from *Influence of the American Revolution on Europe* quoted above, 7, as well as *Fragment on the New Atlantis; or, Combined Efforts of the Human Species for the Advancement of Science* (1793) [*Fragment sur l'Atlantide, ou efforts combinés de l'espèce humaine pour le progrès des sciences*], in *Selected Writings*, 283–300.

59. *Eulogy of Franklin*, 107.

60. *Mirage in the West*, 144–61. Echeverria's book remains the indispensable study of the vast literature on America produced in eighteenth- and early nineteenth-century France.

61. The figure of Franklin was endowed with a significance all the more powerful in that it combined these two fundamental dimensions of the American myth.

62. Bk. 11, chap. 6.

63. By the Seventh Amendment, included in the Bill of Rights (1791).

64. Thirteenth Amendment (1865).

65. Seventeenth Amendment (1913).

66. Twenty-Second Amendment (1951).

67. *Aux citoyens français, sur la nouvelle constitution* (June 1793) [To the citizens of France, on the new constitution], in *Œuvres de Condorcet*, 12:653–75. The Jacobin constitution was never applied, due to the establishment of the revolutionary government.

68. *Sketch for a Historical Picture of the Progress of the Human Mind*, trans. June Barraclough (London: Weidenfeld and Nicolson, 1955), 145, 147.

69. Ibid., 143–44 (emphasis mine; words between brackets are my own corrections to the 1955 translation, which is inaccurate here). The main cause of this contrast between the two revolutions is pointed out in the *Sketch* itself and in the *Lettre de Junius à William Pitt* (1793) [Letter from Junius to William Pitt]: the reason why "the French Revolution was certainly much bloodier than would have been desirable for the happiness and swift emancipation of

humankind" (*Œuvres de Condorcet*, 12:328, my translation), is that "in France, . . . the revolution was to embrace the entire economy of society, change every social relation and find its way down to the furthest links of the political chain" (*Sketch*, 146); on the contrary, "the American Revolution was peaceful, because the people had to change only the distribution of political powers, and every law, every institution, almost every procedure could be preserved" (*Œuvres de Condorcet*, 12:330, my translation).

INFLUENCE OF THE AMERICAN REVOLUTION ON EUROPE

1. Condorcet and Lafayette were close until 1790. Both were founding members of the Société de 1789, a club of moderate reformers active in 1790 and early 1791. The break between the two men occurred in 1791 on the occasion of the king's flight in June and the Champ de Mars massacre in July. As head of the Garde nationale, Lafayette was directly involved in the latter. At that point, Condorcet became a staunch republican, whereas Lafayette moved gradually toward the camp of the counterrevolution.

2. Famous Persian poet of the thirteenth century, much admired by Voltaire, who was one of Condorcet's mentors (along with Turgot and d'Alembert).

3. In 1781 Raynal had established a prize at the Académie de Lyon for the best essay on the following question: "Has the discovery of America been harmful or useful to humankind? If some good has resulted from it, what are the means to preserve and increase it? If it has produced some harm, what are the means to correct it?" He had himself already answered the question rather negatively in the last chapter of his monumental and extremely successful history of European colonization, the *History of the East and West Indies*. See "Reflections upon the good and the evil which the discovery of the New World hath done to Europe," in Guillaume-Thomas Raynal, *A Philosophical and Political History of the Settlements and Trade of the Europeans in the East and West Indies*, 8:366–74.

4. This is a central tenet in Condorcet's political thought: popular government and elections must be conceived of "as a mechanism to reach the truth," and not simply "as indicating the will of the greatest number, that is to say, the will of the strongest." "Discours préliminaire" to *Essai sur l'application de l'analyse à la probabilité des décisions rendues à la pluralité des voix* (1785) [Essay on the application of calculus and probability theory to collective decision-making], in *Sur les élections et autres textes* (Paris: Fayard, 1986), 81 (my translation). It is one of the principal reasons why Condorcet constantly rejects the model of ancient republics and greets with enthusiasm the new American model.

5. We find here the best presentation of natural rights as Condorcet understood them before the French Revolution. As he explains in the following paragraphs, this is a ranking in order of importance, the right to participate in government, and therefore the right to vote, being last. At the time when he wrote these lines, in 1786, Condorcet was not yet a republican, nor was he a supporter of universal suffrage. See *Letters from New Haven*, letter 2, 295–97; and *Ideas on Despotism*, sec. 19. However, his definition of the last among natural rights points clearly in this direction already.

6. In other words, in a free society the rational character of the law is more important than its democratic origin.

7. See the conclusion of *Letters from New Haven*: "You can more easily destroy this inequality [in wealth], or prevent its progress, in America than in Europe, because there are no family distinctions there, nor laws derived from the feudal system and the fortunes of finance. You need only fear the effects of primogeniture and the fortunes built on commerce and banking. The only remedy is freedom of commerce and good civil laws. No other system can prevent unequal fortunes, in which case neither sumptuary laws, nor censors, nor complicated constitutions, nor any of the old political ruses can prevent the rise of social inequal-

ity. Nowhere is a citizen in service, a worker or a farmer the equal of the very rich citizen for whom he works. Nowhere is the poor man with no self-respect the equal of the man who has received a thorough education. There are necessarily two classes of citizen wherever there are very poor people and very rich people, and republican equality cannot exist in any country where the civil, financial and commercial laws allow the existence of enduring large fortunes" (333).

8. Author of a famous *Project for Perpetual Peace in Europe* (1713).

9. A similar optimism regarding the swift abolition of slavery in the United States is expressed in the "Supplement," 47–48, and in *Réflexions sur l'esclavage des nègres* (1781/88) [Reflections on negro slavery], Condorcet's main abolitionist work. See *Réflexions sur l'esclavage des nègres*, ed. Jean-Paul Doguet (Paris: GF-Flammarion, 2009), 89n, 126–28. Condorcet was also a member, and in 1789 the president, of the abolitionist Société des amis des noirs (Society of the friends of black people), founded by Brissot and active between 1788 and 1799. On Condorcet and slavery, see David Williams, "Condorcet and the Abolition of Slavery in the French Colonies," in *Enlightenment and Emancipation*, ed. Susan Manning and Peter France (Lewisburg: Bucknell University Press, 2006), 15–29; Williams, *Condorcet and Modernity*, 139–58; Richard H. Popkin, "Condorcet, Abolitionist," in Rosenfield, *Condorcet Studies I*, 35–47.

10. Close to the physiocrats, and a disciple of Turgot (who appointed him *inspecteur général des monnaies* in 1775), Condorcet was opposed to all restrictions on freedom of trade. See, in particular, his *Lettres sur le commerce des grains* (1775) [Letters on the grain trade], and chapter 4, on trade.

11. The right to vote.

12. This critical allusion is probably aimed at Montesquieu, and perhaps at Rousseau as well (see *The Social Contract*, bk. 3, chaps. 10–11). In *Letters from New Haven*, Condorcet also criticizes "men who maintain that no large free States could ever exist, or that political bodies, like individuals, have a period of youth followed by maturity and then decay and death" (321). The notion that political institutions or governments have only a brief life span inscribed in a cycle of rise, maturity, and decline can be found throughout Montesquieu's works. It appears in the story of the Troglodytes in the *Persian Letters* (1721, letters 11–14), and figures prominently in *Considerations on the Causes of the Greatness of the Romans and Their Decline* (1734) as well as in *The Spirit of the Laws* (1748), where moderate governments, republic and monarchy, always seem threatened with decadence (see, in particular, bk. 8). On England, Montesquieu writes, "Since all human things have an end, the state of which we are speaking will lose its liberty; it will perish. Rome, Lacedaemonia, and Carthage have surely perished. This state will perish when legislative power is more corrupt than executive power." *The Spirit of the Laws*, 166 (bk. 11, chap. 6). Condorcet, whose name would remain so closely associated with the idea of progress, could only be hostile to this dimension of Montesquieu's thought.

13. Like Montesquieu, Condorcet sees England as a blend of monarchy and republic.

14. Notably Voltaire and Diderot. Even among liberals, republicans were extremely rare in France before the Revolution. It was generally agreed that this form of government was appropriate only for very small states. See, for instance, Montesquieu, *The Spirit of the Laws*, bk. 8, chap. 16; and Rousseau, *The Social Contract*, bk. 3, chaps. 3–4, 8.

15. As this and the preceding paragraphs make clear, in the debates at the end of the Old Regime and the beginning of the Revolution between "Anglophiles" (admirers of Montesquieu and of Jean-Louis de Lolme's *Constitution of England*) and "Americanists," Condorcet sided squarely with the latter. See Appleby, "America as a Model for the Radical French Reformers of 1789."

16. Thus the example of the United States supplied the French philosophes with a weapon of crucial importance in their campaign in favor of individual liberties. As Condorcet points out, the American experience shows that freedom of the press and religious liberties do

not undermine social order. Specifically, he has in mind the first and most influential of the American declarations of rights, that of Virginia, which, as early as June 1776, inscribed freedom of the press and freedom of conscience as fundamental human rights (secs. 12 and 16, respectively). See *Ideas on Despotism*, sec. 21.

17. Condorcet is criticizing here two of the most famous theories developed in *The Spirit of the Laws*: the separation and balance of powers (bk. 11), and the influence of climate and esprit général on legislation (bks. 14–19). In both cases, he objects to what he considered Montesquieu's excessive relativism or empiricism. Regarding the balance of powers, the topic of bicameralism particularly attracted his attention. Condorcet was firmly opposed to any division of the legislative power into two chambers, above all to a division into upper and lower houses after the English model of Lords and Commons. In his view, bicameralism is a useless, even dangerous complication, because it is aristocratic in spirit and can cause a paralysis of the legislature. The notion of moderation, so dear to Montesquieu, and the idea of reconciling diverging interests, are fundamentally foreign to Condorcet's political thought. For him, the goal of the legislative process should not be a compromise between different individual or group preferences, but a collective search for truth following the universal principles of reason and justice. Therefore, he favors a strong legislative power concentrated in a single chamber. See the "Supplement," 51–53, and *Eulogy of Franklin*, 95, 101–2, as well as *Letters from New Haven*, letter 4, 325–33; and *Principles of the Constitutional Plan*, 155–62. The same universalism and rationalism naturally lead Condorcet to deny any significant role to the climate and the general spirit in the determination of the law. On this latter point, Condorcet is at odds not only with Montesquieu but also with Rousseau, who had adopted the theory of climate in *The Social Contract* (bk. 3, chap. 8). See *Observations de Condorcet sur le 29e livre de "l'Esprit des lois"* (1780) [Observations by Condorcet on the 29th book of *The Spirit of the Laws*], in *Œuvres de Condorcet*, 1:376–81, specifically the following passage: "Since truth, reason, justice, human rights, the interest of property, liberty and security are the same everywhere, there is no reason why every province of a state, or even every state, should not have the same criminal laws, the same civil laws, the same trade laws, etc. A good law must be good for all men, just as a true proposition is true for all" (378, my translation). See also Baker, *Condorcet*, 220–22, 259–63.

18. Allusion to the remonstrance of the Parlement de Paris against Turgot's edicts of 1776. Among other reforms, these edicts included the abolition of the corvée (unpaid forced labor to which the populace was subject) and the introduction of a new general property tax, whereas traditionally, Old Regime forms of income and property taxes, like the taille, were paid mostly by commoners.

19. Another critical remark directed at Montesquieu, who had singled out honor, exclusive prerogative of the nobility, as the principle of monarchical government. But Condorcet seems to overlook the specific meaning attached to the concept of honor as principle of government in *The Spirit of the Laws*. Like republican virtue, another principle of government, honor as defined by Montesquieu is not to be understood in a general sense, moral or philosophical. It is a class prejudice, useful to the monarchical state, but "speaking philosophically, it is true that the honor that guides all the parts of the state is a false honor." *The Spirit of the Laws*, 27 (bk. 3, chap. 7).

20. Lafayette, who had played a major role in the Virginia campaign and the decisive victory at Yorktown (1781).

21. *Decree of the King's State Council of August 30, 1784, Concerning Foreign Trade in the French Islands of America.*

22. Again, a critical allusion to Montesquieu.

23. This is one of the major conclusions of Condorcet's main work in the field of mathematics applied to political theory, *Essai sur l'application de l'analyse à la probabilité des décisions*

rendues à la pluralité des voix, where he develops a theory of voting based on the calculus of probabilities. Known today as "Condorcet's jury theorem," it can be stated as follows: Suppose a jury or assembly has to choose between two alternatives. Suppose also that members of this assembly all have an identical competence such that they are more likely to be right than wrong (i.e., the probability of the correctness of each member's vote is supposed constant and superior to one-half); then the calculus of probabilities shows that the collective competence of the assembly (the probability that the assembly will render a correct majority decision) is greater than the individual competence of its members, and increases with this individual competence and/or the number of the assembly members. See "Discours préliminaire" to *Essai sur l'application de l'analyse*, 29–46; a partial translation of this text is available as the introduction to *Essay on the Application of Mathematics to the Theory of Decision-Making*, in *Selected Writings*, 33–70 (esp. 48–50, for the jury theorem). The idea of common will as expression of a truth rather than a mere collective choice presents some affinities with the concept of general will (as opposed to the will of all, or the sum of particular wills) in Rousseau's *Social Contract*. See bk. 2, chap. 3 in particular, and Bernard Grofman and Scott L. Feld, "Rousseau's General Will: A Condorcetian Perspective," *American Political Science Review* 82, no. 2 (1988): 567–76; Baker, *Condorcet*, 229–31. But the parallel can be misleading in other respects: while both Rousseau and Condorcet reject the notion of voting as simply expressing preference based on private interest, the communitarian, immediate, and spontaneous character of Rousseau's general will (see, e.g., *The Social Contract*, bk. 4, chap. 1) is very different from voting as Condorcet sees it, as a judgment expressed by autonomous individuals using their reason.

24. In identifying a country's "real wealth" with "the net product of the land," Condorcet seems to follow the economic theories of the physiocrats. At the same time, he diverges from them by asserting that industry and trade, not just agriculture, are also economic activities that generate wealth.

25. Silver: the precious metal itself or a metal currency in silver. Even without considering the special case of international trade, the use of paper currency did not begin to spread until the very late eighteenth and early nineteenth centuries.

26. More precisely, the House of Bourbon, reigning family in France but also in several countries of southern Europe, most notably Spain.

27. This time Rousseau is the intended target. Condorcet is touching on the topic of the positive or negative social impact of luxury, one of the great economic and political debates of the eighteenth century. Montesquieu considered luxury incompatible with the spirit of equality and frugality characteristic of republics, but useful in modern monarchies, where it stimulates commerce. See *The Spirit of the Laws*, bk. 7, chaps. 2 and 4; bk. 20, chap. 4. Voltaire always remained a strong supporter of luxury, inseparable in his view from the progress of civilization. See, e.g., the poem *Le Mondain* (1736) [The man of the world] and the article "Luxury" in the *Philosophical Dictionary* (1764). Rousseau, on the other hand, unambiguously condemned luxury as destructive of equality and good morals. See, in particular, the *Discourse on the Arts and Sciences* (1750) and the *Discourse on the Origin of Inequality* (1755). Finally, in the *History of the East and West Indies*, Raynal and Diderot rarely miss an opportunity to criticize the corrupting influence of luxury. But Diderot makes the distinction between "bad" luxury (ostentation) and "good" (comfort). See *Mémoires for Catherine II* (1773), art. 26; *Observations on the Nakaz* (1774), arts. 306 and 307; *Refutation of Helvétius* (1774), sec. 6. Condorcet's position also keeps clear of the extremes: without condemning luxury in general, he remains concerned about the excessive inequalities it can create. For an excellent recent survey of the question, see Jeremy Jennings, "The Debate About Luxury in Eighteenth- and Nineteenth-Century French Political Thought," *Journal of the History of Ideas* 68, no. 1 (2007): 79–105.

28. Like the physiocrats, Condorcet championed free trade policies: the reduction of state intervention in economic matters and the elimination of restrictions on freedom of trade

(taxes, monopolies, guilds, etc.). He was therefore a harsh critic of mercantilism, whether in its French version inherited from Colbert or in its English form. See the next to last paragraph of this chapter. On Condorcet's economic thought, see Williams, *Condorcet and Modernity*, 225–49; Emma Rothschild, *Economic Sentiments: Adam Smith, Condorcet, and the Enlightenment* (Cambridge: Harvard University Press, 2001); J. Salwyn Schapiro, *Condorcet and the Rise of Liberalism* (New York: Octagon Books, 1963 [1934]), 156–77.

SUPPLEMENT TO FILIPPO MAZZEI'S RESEARCHES ON THE UNITED STATES

1. This supplement appears after *Influence of the American Revolution on Europe*, at the end of the fourth and last volume of Filippo Mazzei's *Recherches historiques et politiques sur les États-Unis de l'Amérique Septentrionale*, 4:284–364. It is not simply an addition to Condorcet's text but to Mazzei's book as a whole. Nevertheless, it is certainly, at least in large part, by Condorcet, and for two essential reasons: first, certain characteristic features of his political thought are easy to recognize in it, notably his opposition to bicameralism and his distrust of a strong executive power; second, it is included in both the Cabanis edition of the *Œuvres complètes de Condorcet* (Brunswick: Vieweg; Paris: Henrichs, 1804) and the Arago edition of the *Œuvres de Condorcet* (Paris: Firmin Didot, 1847), and all Condorcet scholars agree on its authorship. On that last point, see for instance, Dippel, "Condorcet et la discussion des constitutions américaines en France avant 1789," 204; Schapiro, *Condorcet and Liberalism*, 224; Franck Alengry, *Condorcet, guide de la Révolution française, théoricien du droit constitutionnel et précurseur de la science sociale* (Paris: Giard et Brière, 1903), 24.

2. Shays' Rebellion (1786–87), named after its leader, Daniel Shays. As Mazzei and Condorcet explain, the rebels were mostly farmers impoverished by heavy debts and taxes.

3. Like others following, this allusion to a preceding section refers to Mazzei's book, not Condorcet's essay.

4. Mazzei had become an American citizen. Condorcet had been made an honorary freeman of the city of New Haven in 1785.

5. Violent anti-Catholic riots in London in 1780 during which several hundred rioters were killed or wounded by the army.

6. Weavers' strike in Glasgow in 1787.

7. Treaty of Paris (1783).

8. *Pennsylvania Mercury and Universal Advertiser*, No. 110.

9. See Worthington C. Ford et al., eds., *Journals of the Continental Congress, 1774–1789*, 34 vols. (Washington, D.C.: 1904–37), 32:177–84.

10. See Max Farrand, ed., *The Records of the Federal Convention of 1787*, 3 vols. (New Haven: Yale University Press, 1911–37), 2:666–67.

11. Adopted November 15, 1777.

12. This section was modified by the Seventeenth Amendment, ratified in 1913. Since then, senators, like representatives, have been elected by direct popular vote.

13. Only since the ratification of the Twenty-Second Amendment (1951) have presidents been limited to two terms.

14. The king of Poland was elected by the Diet, or general assembly.

15. Head of the executive branch in the former republic of the United Provinces of the Netherlands.

16. Under the Articles of Confederation (article 9), disputes between states were to be settled by an ad hoc special court, appointed by mutual consent or by Congress. The Constitution creates a supreme court and gives it jurisdiction in such cases.

17. The Bill of Rights (1791) did so in the Seventh Amendment.

18. William Pitt the Younger had become head of the British government in 1783 at the age of twenty-four.

19. Another allusion to Lafayette.

20. Condorcet was a fervent advocate of women's rights. See, in particular, *On the Admission of Women to the Rights of Citizenship* (1790) [*Sur l'admission des femmes au droit de cité*], in *Selected Writings*, 97–104 (also translated as *On Giving Women the Right of Citizenship*, in McLean and Hewitt, *Condorcet*, 335–40); and my own study, "Condorcet, Social Mathematics, and Women's Rights," *Eighteenth-Century Studies* 42, no. 3 (Spring 2009): 347–62; as well as Joan Landes, "The History of Feminism: Marie-Jean-Antoine-Nicolas de Caritat, marquis de Condorcet," in *The Stanford Encyclopedia of Philosophy* (Spring 2009 ed.), ed. Edward N. Zalta, http://plato.stanford.edu/archives/spr2009/entries/histfem-condorcet/; Williams, *Condorcet and Modernity*, 158–71; Madelyn Gutwirth, "Civil Rights and the Wrongs of Women," in *A New History of French Literature*, ed. Denis Hollier (Cambridge: Harvard University Press, 1989), 558–66; Barbara Brookes, "The Feminism of Condorcet and Sophie de Grouchy," *Studies on Voltaire and the Eighteenth Century* 189 (1980): 297–361.

21. Cesare Beccaria, Italian jurist, author of the very influential treatise *On Crimes and Punishments* (1764).

22. In a letter to Franklin dated July 8, 1788, Condorcet wrote, "I have seen, my dear and illustrious colleague, your new federal constitution, and the speech you delivered on this occasion. If it had to be written immediately, if it was impossible to arrange it differently, it will have to be counted among necessary evils; and we will have to hope that objections will be strong enough to make a new convention necessary in a few years. I am sorry to see the aristocratic spirit trying to insinuate itself among you despite so many wise precautions." Benjamin Franklin Papers, American Philosophical Society, Philadelphia (my translation).

23. Several versions of this speech exist. Our rendering is based on the abbreviated version quoted by Mazzei and Condorcet and on the full version in Farrand, *The Records of the Federal Convention*, 2:641–43.

24. Because of hyperinflation.

25. Frankland or Franklin, a small state that had declared its independence in 1784. It was never officially recognized and disappeared quickly. It was located in what was at the time western North Carolina, today eastern Tennessee.

IDEAS ON DESPOTISM

1. At the time Condorcet wrote these lines, the royal veto had already disappeared in practice in England; on the other hand, the House of Lords retained its negative right until the beginning of the twentieth century.

2. The House of Commons only became a democratic and representative body with the reforms of the nineteenth century.

3. Notably Montesquieu, of course, for whom "political liberty is found only in moderate governments." *The Spirit of the Laws*, 155 (bk. 11, chap. 4). In Condorcet's view, on the other hand, liberty is best secured when natural rights are guaranteed.

4. Consultative assembly, appointed by the king, who convened it in 1787 and again in 1788. The latter assembly discussed the topic of the representation of the third estate in comparison with the clergy and the nobility at the upcoming Estates General but refused to endorse any reform. At issue was whether the number of representatives of the third estate would be doubled to match the combined number of representatives of the clergy and nobility, and whether voting would be by head in a single assembly instead of separately by estate.

5. The marquis de Mirabeau (father of the comte de Mirabeau), prominent physiocrat, who had published his *Theory of Taxation* in 1760. The work attacked the tax farmers (or tax collectors).

6. Last *contrôleur général des finances* under Louis XV.

7. According to the logic of late eighteenth-century bourgeois liberalism, free competition should guarantee equal opportunity of access to property. Thus a relatively egalitarian society of small property owners would emerge. The later evolution of capitalism, particularly the trend toward ever-greater concentration of capital, revealed the limits of this essentially precapitalist ideal.

8. See, in particular, *The Nature and Purpose of Public Instruction* (1791) [*Nature et objet de l'instruction publique*], in *Selected Writings*, 105–42. On Condorcet and education, see Elaine McAllister, "Condorcet and Jefferson on Education," in *Condorcet Studies II*, ed. David Williams (New York: Peter Lang, 1987), 87–117; Manuela Albertone, "Enlightenment and Revolution: The Evolution of Condorcet's Ideas on Education," in Rosenfield, *Condorcet Studies I*, 131–44; Baker, *Condorcet*, 285–303; Schapiro, *Condorcet and Liberalism*, 196–214.

9. This list appears to be substantially different from the one proposed in *Influence of the American Revolution on Europe* (see "Introduction," above). Here, Condorcet does not specifically mention the right to equality under the law, and he also omits the right to participate in government by voting. Nevertheless, these last two rights are implied under the general right to equality. In his last statement on the subject, Condorcet settled on the following rights: liberty, equality, security, property, social guarantee (of these same rights, by the citizenry as a whole), and resistance to oppression. Under these general categories are notably included freedom of opinion, of worship, and of the press, equality under the law, and the rights to education and to public assistance. See *Plan for a Declaration of the Natural, Civil and Political Rights of Man* (1793) [*Projet de déclaration des droits naturels, civils et politiques des hommes*], in McLean and Hewitt, *Condorcet*, 280–83. The right to vote, extended to all men aged twenty-one and older, is established in the project of constitution itself.

10. Moreover, if one accepts the liberal ideal of a relatively egalitarian society of small property owners based on equal opportunity of access to property guaranteed by free competition, then the private interests of property owners would coincide with the public good. And equal access to property would also mean equal access to voting rights. Condorcet will only become an advocate of universal suffrage during the republican phase of the French Revolution. See *Principles of the Constitutional Plan*, 165–68.

11. June 12, to be exact.

12. George Mason. The Virginia Declaration of Rights is indeed the first declaration of human rights in the modern sense. It was a major influence on the Declaration of Independence and the Bill of Rights.

13. Tax per head, without regard to property or income.

14. See note 19 to *Examen du gouvernement d'Angleterre* in the appendix, and also the conclusion of note 22 (these two notes are probably by Dupont de Nemours):

The people of the United States of America are the first, and so far the only nation, to have recognized that a legislation must not begin with *a contract*, like one between enemies making compromises and coming to an agreement, but with *the statement of the principle of all contracts*, as do wise men who first examine what the essence of the question is.

Thereafter, the nation's delegates can no longer be told, *You will have such and such authority, you will act arbitrarily up to such and such point*, with limits carefully set that are always easy to evade with skill or exceed by force. They are simply told, *You will see that each and every citizen's rights are respected*. And, *all men have such and such right*. As soon as this is said and understood, every right becomes the responsibility of every man.

It is impossible for an imperfect constitution or bad laws to last long in a state where humankind is endowed with a good *declaration of rights*. It is impossible for a good declaration of rights in a single corner of the world not to become universal law.

He who first imagined thus laying down such fundamental laws deserves the most honorable of statues among the leading benefactors of the human race.

The declarations of rights adopted by the various United States of America are neither complete nor methodical enough; but all the truths they contain are beyond doubt. The stroke of genius is to have put them forward. Now, reason and logic are enough to develop their consequences, go back to their true principles, and arrange both in methodical order. It is possible to achieve such a degree of perfection in this matter that in the whole world there could not be two declarations of rights differing by a single word. What will become of arbitrary governments then? (199–201, my translation).

EULOGY OF FRANKLIN

1. Franklin had become a member of the French Academy of Sciences in 1772. Condorcet had been its permanent secretary since 1776. The epigraph translates to "He seized lightning from the sky, then scepters from tyrants." Franklin's birth date was actually January 17, 1706 (January 6, 1705, in the old Julian calendar). On the eulogies, see David Williams, "Condorcet and the Art of Eulogy," in *Voltaire and His World*, ed. R. J. Howells, Adrienne Mason, Haydn Mason, and David Williams (Oxford: Voltaire Foundation, 1985), 363–80; Charles B. Paul, *Science and Immortality: The "Éloges" of the Paris Academy of Sciences (1699–1791)* (Berkeley: University of California Press, 1980).

2. Seventeen, in fact; Benjamin was the fifteenth.

3. Famous English journal published by Joseph Addison and Richard Steele in 1711–12 and 1714, instrumental in spreading the spirit of the Enlightenment and in consolidating the public sphere as described by Jürgen Habermas (see also note 11, below).

4. Anthony Collins (1676–1729), deist and materialist thinker, friend of Locke.

5. William Wollaston published his *Religion of Nature Delineated* in 1722. A second edition appeared in 1724.

6. Bernard de Mandeville (1670–1733), author of *The Fable of the Bees*.

7. William Lyons, surgeon who moved in intellectual circles inclined toward skepticism.

8. Henry Pemberton (1694–1771), physician, mathematician and man of letters, friend and collaborator of Newton.

9. Sir Hans Sloane (1660–1753), physician and naturalist, future president of the Royal Society and founder of the British Museum.

10. The *Pennsylvania Gazette*.

11. Here we have an excellent definition of the appropriate role and structure of the public sphere, what it should and should not be, according to late eighteenth-century bourgeois liberalism. It is surprising that Habermas, in *The Structural Transformation of the Public Sphere*, never mentions Condorcet, who represents in many respects a paradigmatic figure illustrating his thesis.

12. In 1747, more accurately.

13. The Seven Years' War (1756–63), known in North America as the French and Indian War, which in fact began as early as 1754.

14. The Stamp Act (1765).

15. This appointment dates back to 1753, in fact.

16. During the Old Regime, arbitrary orders (of imprisonment, for example) signed by the king.

17. John Wilkes, radical English politician and journalist. He was charged with seditious libel in 1763 for criticizing the ministry and the king.

18. The original constitution of Pennsylvania (1776) was indeed remarkable for being radically democratic. Not only did it concentrate the legislative power in a single chamber of

representatives elected by direct popular vote, but it entrusted the executive power to an executive council consisting of twelve members, also elected. As Condorcet mentions, it was replaced in 1790 by a bicameral system, with a governor as head of the executive. A legislative branch consisting of only one chamber and an elected executive council are also essential features of the constitutional plan presented to the Convention by Condorcet in February 1793. See *Principles of the Constitutional Plan*, 155–65.

19. The Battle of Quebec (1775), an early American defeat in the Revolutionary War.

20. Spain had ceded Gibraltar to Great Britain in 1713, at the end of the War of the Spanish Succession (via the Treaty of Utrecht). The Treaty of Paris (1763), which ended the Seven Years' War, had established a British commissioner in the northern French port of Dunkirk. This commissioner was expelled in 1783, after the victory of the allies in America.

21. The Battle of Saratoga (1777).

22. The Treaty of Alliance (1778).

23. It is thought that during Roman triumphs, the role of the slave who accompanied the victorious emperor or general on his chariot was to remind him frequently that he was only a mere mortal.

24. More precisely, Franklin was president of the Supreme Executive Council of Pennsylvania from 1785 to 1788.

25. See the "Supplement," 59–60 above.

26. An extreme form of skepticism.

27. *Rules by Which a Great Empire May Be Reduced to a Small One* and *An Edict by the King of Prussia*, two satirical pamphlets from 1773.

28. The first English Revolution (1640–60: civil war, execution of Charles I, Commonwealth and Protectorate under Cromwell) and the Glorious Revolution of 1688 (which overthrew James II, a Roman Catholic, to place jointly on the throne William of Orange and his wife, Mary, daughter of James II but a Protestant like her husband). This second revolution also marks the true instauration of a constitutional monarchy in England.

29. In this last paragraph, Condorcet is attacking Rousseau and all those who regarded the sciences and the arts as destructive of virtue and equality and therefore as dangerous to political freedom. The false choice he is denouncing is between science, wrongly considered an obstacle to political freedom, and liberty, wrongly construed on the model of communitarian and virtuous simplicity provided by ancient republics. A false choice, Condorcet believes, since Science and Liberty are the two pillars of the Enlightenment, two inseparable aspects of the same process of human emancipation.

APPENDIX

1. "From nature, justice, order and the laws. From man, judgment, government and punishment."

2. François Quesnay (1694–1774), leader of the physiocratic school.

3. "Nowadays, we tend to model everything on ancient times, and few people have appreciated the great benefits of the invention of the printing press, which gives men who are far apart the ability to discuss matters calmly. At the same time, it removes the influence of eloquence, which can often mislead, and increases that of reason, which never deceives." *Letters from New Haven*, 321.

4. The title pages of *Observations on Government* and *Examen du gouvernement d'Angleterre* state, respectively, "By a farmer, of New Jersey," and "Par un cultivateur de New Jersey."

5. We quote, with modernized spelling, from John Stevens, *Observations on Government, Including Some Animadversions on Mr. Adams's "Defence of the Constitutions of Government of the*

United States of America": And on Mr. De Lolme's "Constitution of England" (New York: W. Ross, 1787), 53.

6. Ibid.

7. Ibid., 54.

8. Ibid., 53.

9. Meaning here the English constitution.

10. As the full title indicates (see note 5 above), *Observations on Government* is essentially a critique of John Adams's *A Defence of the Constitutions of Government of the United States of America* (1787) and Jean-Louis de Lolme's *The Constitution of England* (1771).

11. *Observations on Government*, 33.

12. Ibid., 24.

13. "Supplement," 57 above.

14. This description is not quite accurate with respect to the election of the vice president. Moreover, this electoral procedure was slightly modified by the Twelfth Amendment (1804), requiring notably that the electors distinguish their vote for president from their vote for vice president.

15. This is the minimum requirement for ratification of the Constitution itself (article 7); the minimum requirement for ratification of amendments is approval by three-fourths of the states (article 5).

16. The right of veto enjoyed by every member of the Polish Diet.

SELECTED BIBLIOGRAPHY IN ENGLISH

TRANSLATIONS OF WORKS BY CONDORCET

Condorcet: Foundations of Social Choice and Political Theory. Translated and edited by Iain McLean
and Fiona Hewitt. Aldershot, U.K.: Edward Elgar, 1994. This volume includes the following works:

 *A General Survey of Science—Concerning the Application of Calculus to the Political and Moral
  Sciences.*

 On Ballot Votes.

 "Preliminary Discussion" to *An Essay on the Application of Probability Theory to Plurality
  Decision-Making* (selections).

 On the Constitution and the Functions of Provincial Assemblies (selections).

 On the Form of Elections.

 A Survey of the Principles Underlying the Draft Constitution (1793).

 Outline for the French Constitution (1793).

 On Elections.

 Declaration of Rights (1789).

 On the Need for the Citizens to Ratify the Constitution (1789).

 Plan for a Declaration of the Natural, Civil and Political Rights of Man (1793).

 Condorcet's Advice to His Daughter.

 Condorcet's Testament.

 *Letters from a Freeman of New Haven to a Citizen of Virginia on the Futility of Dividing the
  Legislative Power Among Several Bodies.*

 On Giving Women the Right of Citizenship.

 Rules for the Society of the Friends of Negroes.

 On Admitting the Delegates of the Planters of San Domingo to the National Assembly.

Selected Writings. Edited by Keith M. Baker. Indianapolis: Bobbs-Merrill, 1976. This volume
includes the following works:

 Reception Speech at the French Academy (selections).

 "Introduction" to *Essay on the Application of Mathematics to the Theory of Decision-Making*
  (selections).

 On the Influence of the American Revolution on Europe (introduction and chapter 1).

 Essay on the Constitution and Functions of the Provincial Assemblies (postscript).

 On the Society of 1789.

 On the Admission of Women to the Rights of Citizenship.

 The Nature and Purpose of Public Instruction.

 On the Principles of the Constitutional Plan Presented to the National Convention (1793)
  (abridged).

 A General View of the Science of Social Mathematics.

 Sketch for a Historical Picture of the Progress of the Human Mind (introduction, ninth and
  tenth stages).

 Fragment on the New Atlantis (abridged).

Sketch for a Historical Picture of the Progress of the Human Mind. Translated by June Barraclough.
London: Weidenfeld and Nicolson, 1955.

"*Sketch for a Historical Picture of the Progress of the Human Mind:* Tenth Epoch." Translated by Keith M. Baker. *Daedalus* 133, no. 3 (2004): 65–82.

OTHER RELEVANT PRIMARY SOURCES

Adams, John. 1787. *A Defence of the Constitutions of Government of the United States of America.* 3 vols. New York: Da Capo Press, 1971.

Brissot de Warville, Jacques-Pierre. 1791. *New Travels in the United States of America.* Translated by Mara S. Vamos and Durand Echeverria. Cambridge: Harvard University Press, 1964.

Chastellux, François-Jean, marquis de. 1786. *Travels in North America.* Translated by Howard C. Rice. 2 vols. Chapel Hill: University of North Carolina Press, 1963.

Constant, Benjamin. 1814. *The Spirit of Conquest and Usurpation and Their Relation to European Civilization.* In *Political Writings,* translated and edited by Biancamaria Fontana, 45–167. Cambridge: Cambridge University Press, 1988.

———. 1819. "The Liberty of the Ancients Compared with That of the Moderns." In *Political Writings,* translated and edited by Biancamaria Fontana, 309–28. Cambridge: Cambridge University Press, 1988.

Crèvecœur, J. Hector St. John de. 1782. *Letters from an American Farmer.* Edited by Albert E. Stone. Harmondsworth, U.K.: Penguin, 1981.

Farrand, Max, ed. *The Records of the Federal Convention of 1787.* 3 vols. New Haven: Yale University Press, 1911–37.

Franklin, Benjamin. 1791, 1732–58. *Autobiography, Poor Richard, and Later Writings.* Edited by J. A. Leo Lemay. New York: Library of America, 1997.

Lolme, Jean-Louis de. 1771. *The Constitution of England.* Edited by David Lieberman. Indianapolis: Liberty Fund, 2007.

Mably, Gabriel Bonnot de, Abbé. 1784. *Remarks Concerning the Government and the Laws of the United States of America.* New York: Burt Franklin, 1968.

Mazzei, Philip. 1788. *Researches on the United States.* Translated and edited by Constance D. Sherman. Charlottesville: University Press of Virginia, 1976.

Montesquieu, Charles-Louis de Secondat, baron de. 1748. *The Spirit of the Laws.* Translated and edited by A. M. Cohler, B. C. Miller, and H. S. Stone. Cambridge: Cambridge University Press, 1989.

Pauw, Cornelius de. 1768. *Selections from "Les recherches philosophiques sur les Américains" of M. Pauw: By Mr. W***.* Bath: R. Cruttwell, 1789.

Raynal, Guillaume-Thomas, Abbé. 1780. *A History of the Two Indies.* Translated and edited by Peter Jimack. Aldershot, U.K.: Ashgate, 2006 (selections).

———. 1780. *A Philosophical and Political History of the Settlements and Trade of the Europeans in the East and West Indies.* Translated by John O. Justamond. 8 vols. London: W. Strahan & T. Cadell, 1783. Reprint, 6 vols. New York: Negro Universities Press, 1969.

———. 1780. *The Revolution of America.* Boston: Gregg Press, 1972.

Rousseau, Jean-Jacques. 1762. *The Social Contract, and Other Later Political Writings.* Translated and edited by Victor Gourevitch. Cambridge: Cambridge University Press, 1997.

Stevens, John. *Observations on Government, Including Some Animadversions on Mr. Adams's "Defence of the Constitutions of Government of the United States of America": And on Mr. De Lolme's "Constitution of England."* New York: W. Ross, 1787.

SECONDARY SOURCES

Albertone, Manuela. "Enlightenment and Revolution: The Evolution of Condorcet's Ideas on Education." In *Condorcet Studies I,* edited by Leonora C. Rosenfield, 131–44. Atlantic Highlands, N.J.: Humanities Press, 1984.

Albertone, Manuela, and Antonino De Francesco, eds. *Rethinking the Atlantic World: Europe and America in the Age of Democratic Revolutions*. Houndmills, U.K.: Palgrave Macmillan, 2009.

Aldridge, Alfred O. "Condorcet, Paine, and Historical Method." In *Condorcet Studies I*, edited by Leonora C. Rosenfield, 49–60. Atlantic Highlands, N.J.: Humanities Press, 1984.

———. *Franklin and His French Contemporaries*. New York: New York University Press, 1957.

Ansart, Guillaume. "Condorcet, Social Mathematics, and Women's Rights." *Eighteenth-Century Studies* 42, no. 3 (Spring 2009): 347–62.

———. "Variations on Montesquieu: Raynal and Diderot's *Histoire des deux Indes* and the American Revolution." *Journal of the History of Ideas* 70, no. 3 (2009): 399–420.

Appleby, Joyce. "America as a Model for the Radical French Reformers of 1789." *William and Mary Quarterly* 28, no. 2 (1971): 267–86.

Baker, Keith M. "Condorcet." In *A Critical Dictionary of the French Revolution*, edited by François Furet and Mona Ozouf, translated by Arthur Goldhammer, 204–12. Cambridge: Harvard University Press, 1989.

———. *Condorcet: From Natural Philosophy to Social Mathematics*. Chicago: University of Chicago Press, 1975.

———. "Defining the Public Sphere in Eighteenth-Century France: Variations on a Theme by Habermas." In *Habermas and the Public Sphere*, edited by Craig Calhoun, 181–211. Cambridge, Mass.: MIT Press, 1992.

———. "Political Languages of the French Revolution." In *The Cambridge History of Eighteenth-Century Political Thought*, edited by Mark Goldie and Robert Wokler, 626–59. Cambridge: Cambridge University Press, 2006.

Brookes, Barbara. "The Feminism of Condorcet and Sophie de Grouchy." *Studies on Voltaire and the Eighteenth Century* 189 (1980): 297–361.

Echeverria, Durand. 1957. *Mirage in the West: A History of the French Image of American Society to 1815*. New York: Octagon Books, 1966.

Furet, François, and Mona Ozouf, eds. *A Critical Dictionary of the French Revolution*. Translated by Arthur Goldhammer. Cambridge: Harvard University Press, 1989.

Gerbi, Antonello. *The Dispute of the New World: The History of a Polemic, 1750–1900*. Translated by Jeremy Moyle. Pittsburgh: University of Pittsburgh Press, 1973.

Grofman, Bernard, and Scott L. Feld. "Rousseau's General Will: A Condorcetian Perspective." *American Political Science Review* 82, no. 2 (1988): 567–76.

Gutwirth, Madelyn. "Civil Rights and the Wrongs of Women." In *A New History of French Literature*, edited by Denis Hollier, 558–66. Cambridge: Harvard University Press, 1989.

Habermas, Jürgen. *The Structural Transformation of the Public Sphere: An Inquiry into a Category of Bourgeois Society*. Translated by Thomas Burger with Frederick Lawrence. Cambridge, Mass.: MIT Press, 1989.

Jennings, Jeremy. "The Debate About Luxury in Eighteenth- and Nineteenth-Century French Political Thought." *Journal of the History of Ideas* 68, no. 1 (2007): 79–105.

Landes, Joan. "The History of Feminism: Marie-Jean-Antoine-Nicolas de Caritat, marquis de Condorcet." In *The Stanford Encyclopedia of Philosophy*. Spring 2009 edition. Edited by Edward N. Zalta. http://plato.stanford.edu/archives/spr2009/entries/histfem-condorcet/.

Lutz, Donald S. "The Relative Influence of European Writers on Late Eighteenth-Century American Political Thought." *American Political Science Review* 78, no. 1 (1984): 189–97.

Manin, Bernard. "Montesquieu." In *A Critical Dictionary of the French Revolution*, edited by François Furet and Mona Ozouf, translated by Arthur Goldhammer, 728–41. Cambridge: Harvard University Press, 1989.

McAllister, Elaine. "Condorcet and Jefferson on Education." In *Condorcet Studies II*, edited by David Williams, 87–117. New York: Peter Lang, 1987.

McLean, Iain, and Fiona Hewitt. "Condorcet and the Americans: Bicameralism and the Separation of Powers." In *Condorcet: Foundations of Social Choice and Political Theory*, edited and translated by Iain McLean and Fiona Hewitt, 64–69. Aldershot, U.K.: Edward Elgar, 1994.

McLean, Iain, and Arnold B. Urken. "Did Jefferson or Madison Understand Condorcet's Theory of Social Choice?" *Public Choice* 73, no. 4 (1992): 445–57.

Mintz, Max M. "Condorcet's Reconsideration of America as a Model for Europe." *Journal of the Early Republic* 11, no. 4 (1991): 493–506.

Paul, Charles B. *Science and Immortality: The "Éloges" of the Paris Academy of Sciences (1699–1791)*. Berkeley: University of California Press, 1980.

Popkin, Richard H. "Condorcet, Abolitionist." In *Condorcet Studies I*, edited by Leonora C. Rosenfield, 35–47. Atlantic Highlands, N.J.: Humanities Press, 1984.

Raynaud, Philippe. "American Revolution." In *A Critical Dictionary of the French Revolution*, edited by François Furet and Mona Ozouf, translated by Arthur Goldhammer, 593–603. Cambridge: Harvard University Press, 1989.

Rosenblum, Victor G. "Condorcet as Constitutional Draftsman." In *Condorcet Studies I*, edited by Leonora C. Rosenfield, 187–205. Atlantic Highlands, N.J.: Humanities Press, 1984.

Rosenfield, Leonora C., ed. *Condorcet Studies I*. Atlantic Highlands, N.J.: Humanities Press, 1984.

Rosenkranz, Nicholas Q. "Condorcet and the Constitution: A Response to *The Law of Other States*." *Stanford Law Review* 59, no. 5 (March 2007): 1281–308.

Rothschild, Emma. *Economic Sentiments: Adam Smith, Condorcet, and the Enlightenment*. Cambridge: Harvard University Press, 2001.

Schapiro, J. Salwyn. 1934. *Condorcet and the Rise of Liberalism*. New York: Octagon Books, 1963.

Schofield, Norman. "The Intellectual Contribution of Condorcet to the Founding of the U.S. Republic, 1785–1800." *Social Choice and Welfare* 25, nos. 2/3 (2005): 303–18.

———. "Madison, Jefferson, and Condorcet." In *Architects of Political Change: Constitutional Quandaries and Social Choice Theory*, 98–134. Cambridge: Cambridge University Press, 2006.

Urken, Arnold B. "The Condorcet-Jefferson Connection and the Origins of Social Choice Theory." *Public Choice* 72, nos. 2/3 (1991): 213–36.

Williams, David. *Condorcet and Modernity*. Cambridge: Cambridge University Press, 2004.

———. "Condorcet and the Abolition of Slavery in the French Colonies." In *Enlightenment and Emancipation*, edited by Susan Manning and Peter France, 15–29. Lewisburg: Bucknell University Press, 2006.

———. "Condorcet and the Art of Eulogy." In *Voltaire and His World*, edited by R. J. Howells, Adrienne Mason, Haydn Mason, and David Williams, 363–80. Oxford: Voltaire Foundation, 1985.

———, ed. *Condorcet Studies II*. New York: Peter Lang, 1987.

INDEX OF PROPER NAMES

Adams, John, 49, 115, 125 n. 5, 139 n. 10
Addison, Joseph, 13, 137 n. 3
Albertone, Manuela, 136 n. 8
Aldridge, Alfred O., 128–29 n. 48
Alembert, Jean le Rond d', 130 n. 2
Alengry, Franck, 134 n. 1
Ansart, Guillaume, 126 n. 12, 135 n. 20
Appleby, Joyce, 126 n. 9, 131 n. 15

Baker, Keith M., 5, 125–26 n. 6, 126 n. 11, 132 n. 17, 132–33 n. 23, 136 n. 8
Barraclough, June, 129 n. 68
Beccaria, Cesare, 57, 135 n. 21
Blair, John, 50
Boyle, Robert, 106
Braddock, Edward (General), 90
Brissot de Warville, Jacques-Pierre, 1–2, 125 n. 1, 131 n. 9
Brookes, Barbara, 135 n. 20
Buffon, Georges-Louis Leclerc (comte de), 128 n. 31
Burger, Thomas, 129 n. 49

Calhoun, Craig, 126 n. 11
Carleton, Guy (Sir), 48
Carmarthen, Francis Osborne (Duke of Leeds, Marquess of), 49
Catherine II (Empress of Russia), 133 n. 27
Charles I (King of England), 91 n. v, 138 n. 28
Chastellux, François-Jean de Beauvoir (marquis de), 1, 125 n. 1
Chouillet, Anne-Marie, 128 n. 34
Cohler, Anne M., 127 n. 29
Colbert, Jean-Baptiste, 133–34 n. 28
Coleman, William, 81
Collins, Anthony, 80, 137 n. 4
Comte, Auguste, 126 n. 7
Condorcet, Marie-Jean-Antoine-Nicolas Caritat (marquis de),
  Eulogy of Franklin, 13–19, 79–107, 128 n. 42, 132 n. 17
  Fragment on the New Atlantis; or, Combined Efforts of the Human Species for the Advancement of Science, 129 n. 58
  Ideas on Despotism, 8, 63–78, 109, 127 n. 16, 128 n. 41, 130 n. 5, 131–32 n. 16
  Influence of the American Revolution on Europe, 4–10, 16, 21–42, 125 n. 3, 128 nn. 45–46, 129 n. 58, 134 n. 1, 136 n. 9
  "Introduction" to *Essay on the Application of Mathematics to the Theory of Decision-Making*, 129 n. 57, 130 n. 4, 132–33 n. 23
  Letter from Junius to William Pitt, 129–30 n. 69
  Letters from a citizen of the United States to a Frenchman on current affairs, 127 n. 15
  Letters from a Freeman of New Haven to a Citizen of Virginia on the Futility of Dividing the Legislative Power Among Several Bodies, 6, 125 n. 3, 128 nn. 37, 44, 130 n. 5, 130–31 n. 7, 131 n. 12, 132 n. 17, 138 n. 3
  Letters on the grain trade, 131 n. 10
  "Notes" to John Stevens's *Observations on Government*, 11–13, 109–18, 127 n. 25, 128 nn. 39, 47, 136–37 n. 14
  Observations by Condorcet on the 29th book of *The Spirit of the Laws*, 132 n. 17
  On the Admission of Women to the Rights of Citizenship, 135 n. 20
  On the Principles of the Constitutional Plan Presented to the National Convention (1793), 125–26 n. 6, 128 nn. 43–44, 132 n. 17, 136 n. 10, 137–38 n. 18
  Plan for a Declaration of the Natural, Civil and Political Rights of Man (1793), 136 n. 9
  Reception Speech at the French Academy, 129 n. 57
  Reflections on negro slavery, 131 n. 9
  Sketch for a Historical Picture of the Progress of the Human Mind, 20, 129 n. 68, 129–30 n. 69
  "Supplement" to Filippo Mazzei's *Researches on the United States*, 10–11, 43–62, 109, 114 n. i, 115–16, 118 n. vi, 127 n. 25, 131 n. 9, 132 n. 17, 138 n. 25
  The Nature and Purpose of Public Instruction, 136 n. 8
  To the citizens of France, on the new constitution (1793), 129 n. 67
Constant, Benjamin, 4, 10, 126 n. 7

Crépel, Pierre, 128 n. 34
Crèvecœur, J. Hector St. John de, 1, 6, 10, 125 n. 1
Cromwell, Oliver, 106, 138 n. 28

Diderot, Denis, 6–7, 9–10, 18–19, 125 n. 2, 126 n. 12, 131 n. 14, 133 n. 27
Dippel, Horst, 128 n. 34, 134 n. 1
Doguet, Jean-Paul, 131 n. 9
Dupont de Nemours, Pierre-Samuel, 109–11, 125 n. 1, 127 n. 25, 128 n. 47, 136–37 n. 14

Echeverria, Durand, 18, 125 n. 4, 129 n. 60

Farrand, Max, 134 n. 10, 135 n. 23
Fauchet, Claude (abbé), 128–29 n. 48
Feld, Scott L., 132–33 n. 23
Folger, Abiah, 79
Fontana, Biancamaria, 126 n. 7
Ford, Worthington C., 134 n. 9
Fox, Charles James, 70
France, Peter, 131 n. 9
Franklin, Benjamin, 2, 13–18, 35, 58–61, 79–107, 127 n. 23, 129 n. 61, 135 n. 22
Franklin, Josiah, 79
Furet, François, 125–26 n. 6, 126 nn. 9, 11

Gauvin-Gallois, Jean-Antoine, 109, 127 n. 25
George II (King of England), 89, 91, 137 n. 15
George III (King of England), 91, 137 n. 17
Gerbi, Antonello, 128 n. 31
Goldhammer, Arthur, 125–26 n. 6
Goldie, Mark, 126 n. 11
Gordon, George (Lord), 46, 134 n. 5
Grace, Robert, 81
Grofman, Bernard, 132–33 n. 23
Grouchy, Sophie de (marquise de Condorcet), 126 n. 7, 135 n. 20
Gutwirth, Madelyn, 135 n. 20

Habermas, Jürgen, 126 n. 11, 129 n. 49, 137 nn. 3, 11
Helvétius, Claude-Adrien, 133 n. 27
Hewitt, Fiona, 125–26 n. 6, 127 n. 20, 128 n. 37, 135 n. 20, 136 n. 9
Hollier, Denis, 135 n. 20
Howells, Robin J., 137 n. 1

James II (King of England), 138 n. 28
Jefferson, Thomas, 2, 127 n. 25, 136 n. 8
Jennings, Jeremy, 133 n. 27
Jimack, Peter, 125 n. 2
Justamond, John O., 125 n. 2

Knox, John, 106

Lafayette, Gilbert du Motier (marquis de), 2–3, 21, 30, 56, 98 n. xi, 125 n. 1, 130 n. 1, 132 n. 20, 135 n. 19
La Ferté, Marie-Isabelle-Gabrielle-Angélique de La Mothe-Houdancourt (duchesse de), 60 n. vii
Landes, Joan, 135 n. 20
Laplace, Pierre-Simon, 126 n. 7
La Rochefoucauld d'Enville, Louis-Alexandre (duc de), 125 n. 1, 128–29 n. 48
Lawrence, Frederick, 129 n. 49
Lawrence, Thomas, 85
Le Veillard, Louis-Guillaume, 100
Lincoln, Benjamin (General), 44
Livingston, William, 109, 127 n. 25
Locke, John, 137 n. 4
Lolme, Jean-Louis de, 4, 115, 131 n. 15, 139 n. 10
Louis XIV (King of France), 90 n. iv
Louis XV (King of France), 135 n. 6
Louis XVI (King of France), 132 n. 21, 135 n. 4
Lutz, Donald S., 126 n. 8
Lyons, William, 81, 137 n. 7

Mably, Gabriel Bonnot de (abbé), 2, 125 n. 3
Madison, James, 50
Mandeville, Bernard de, 81, 137 n. 6
Manin, Bernard, 126 n. 9
Manning, Susan, 131 n. 9
Mary II (Queen of England), 138 n. 28
Mason, Adrienne, 137 n. 1
Mason, George, 50, 136 n. 12
Mason, Haydn, 137 n. 1
Mazzei, Filippo, 2, 10, 43–62, 109, 112–18, 125 n. 3, 127 n. 25
McAllister, Elaine, 136 n. 8
McClurg, James, 50
McLean, Iain, 125–26 n. 6, 127 n. 20, 128 n. 37, 135 n. 20, 136 n. 9
Miller, Basia Carolyn, 127 n. 29
Mintz, Max M., 128 n. 37
Mirabeau, Honoré-Gabriel Riqueti (comte de), 47, 128–29 n. 48, 135 n. 5
Mirabeau, Victor Riqueti (marquis de), 70, 135 n. 5
Montesquieu, Charles-Louis de Secondat (baron de), 3–4, 6–9, 11–12, 19, 25, 81, 126 nn. 8–9, 12, 127 nn. 22, 29, 128 n. 31, 131 nn. 12–15, 132 nn. 17, 19, 22, 133 n. 27, 135 n. 3
Moyle, Jeremy, 128 n. 31

Newton, Isaac (Sir), 106, 137 n. 8

Ozouf, Mona, 125–26 n. 6, 126 nn. 9, 11

Paine, Thomas, 2, 127 n. 25
Palmer, Samuel, 80
Paul, Charles B., 137 n. 1
Pauw, Cornelius de, 128 n. 31
Pémberton, Henry, 81, 137 n. 8
Phocion, 99
Pitt, William (the Younger), 56, 70,
    129–30 n. 69, 134 n. 18
Poisson, Siméon-Denis, 126 n. 7
Popkin, Richard H., 131 n. 9
Prynne, William, 106
Pythagoras, 15, 85

Quesnay, François, 110, 138 n. 2

Randolph, Edmund, 50
Raynal, Guillaume-Thomas (abbé), 1–2, 4,
    6–7, 9–10, 18–19, 21, 125 nn. 2–3,
    126 n. 12, 130 n. 3, 133 n. 27
Robespierre, Maximilien de, 4
Rochambeau, Jean-Baptiste-Donatien de
    Vimeur (comte de), 1
Rosenblum, Victor G., 125–26 n. 6
Rosenfield, Leonora C., 125–26 n. 6, 131 n. 9,
    136 n. 8
Rothschild, Emma, 133–34 n. 28
Rousseau, Jean-Jacques, 3–4, 6, 19, 131 nn. 12,
    14, 132 n. 17, 132–33 n. 23, 133 n. 27,
    138 n. 29

Saadi, 21, 130 n. 2
Saint-Clair, Arthur, 50
Saint-Pierre, Charles-Irénée Castel (abbé de),
    24, 30–31, 131 n. 8
Saint-Simon, Henri de Rouvroy (comte de),
    126 n. 7
Schapiro, J. Salwyn, 133–34 n. 28, 134 n. 1,
    136 n. 8

Scipio ("Africanus"), 56
Shaftesbury, Anthony Ashley Cooper (Earl of),
    80
Shays, Daniel, 43–47
Shepard, William (General), 44
Sherman, Constance D., 125 n. 3
Sieyès, Emmanuel-Joseph (abbé), 106 n. xv
Sloane, Hans (Sir), 81, 137 n. 9
Smith, Adam, 133–34 n. 28
Socrates, 15, 99, 104
Staal, Marguerite de Launay (baronne de),
    60 n. vii
Stanhope, Charles (Earl), 70
Steele, Richard, 13, 137 n. 3
Stevens, John, 109, 112–13, 115, 127 n. 25,
    138 n. 4, 138–39 n. 5
Stone, Harold Samuel, 127 n. 29

Terray, Joseph-Marie (abbé), 71, 135 n. 6
Tocqueville, Alexis de, 126 n. 7, 127 n. 21,
    129 n. 55
Turgot, Anne-Robert-Jacques, 3, 5, 79, 130 n.
    2, 131 n. 10, 132 n. 18

Vicq d'Azyr, Félix, 128–29 n. 48
Voltaire, 7, 15, 25 n. i, 34, 81, 84, 130 n. 2,
    131 n. 14, 133 n. 27

Washington, George, 50, 60–61, 117
Wielhorski, Michel (comte), 118
Wilkes, John, 93, 137 n. 17
William III (King of England), 138 n. 28
Williams, David, 125–26 n. 6, 131 n. 9, 133–34
    n. 28, 135 n. 20, 136 n. 8, 137 n. 1
Wilson, James, 114–15
Wokler, Robert, 126 n. 11
Wollaston, William, 80, 137 n. 5
Wythe, George, 50

Xenophon, 104

Zalta, Edward N., 135 n. 20